HOME OF THE RED MAN

Indian North America Before Columbus

By ROBERT SILVERBERG

NEW YORK GRAPHIC SOCIETY
Publishers, Ltd.
Greenwich, Connecticut

To Margaret C. Scoggin

DRAWINGS BY JUDITH ANN LAWRENCE
MAPS BY RAFAEL PALACIOS

Library of Congress Catalog No. 63–19941
© New York Graphic Society, Publishers, Ltd. 1963
All rights reserved.

Published simultaneously in Canada by
McClelland & Stewart Ltd., Toronto

Printed by Mahony & Roese, New York
Bound by The Book Press, Brattleboro, Vt.

CONTENTS

71- 8679

1

TO A WORLD
UNKNOWN

AT TWO IN THE MORNING ON OCTOBER 12, 1492, THE boom of a cannon shattered the peaceful Caribbean stillness. A Genoese sea captain named Cristoforo Colombo had sighted land that moonlit night, after a five-week journey westward in three small ships, the *Nina*, the *Pinta*, the *Santa Maria*. The cannon shot that thundered from the *Pinta's* deck was the signal. "*Tierra!*" cried the weary seamen. "*Tierra!*" Land!

With the firing of that shot, a world came to its end and a new world was born.

The world that ended that night was the world of the red man. Although the mopping-up operation was to take some four hundred years, the red man's doom was sealed from that moment of discovery. For thousands of years, the people of the Western Hemisphere had dwelt in isolation, according to their various ways. But all that would end now. Wave after wave of white-skinned invaders would come westward—some seeking gold, others furs, others spices, others simply a

1

place to live in peace—and the red man would have to fall back in defeat before that unstoppable tide.

Colombo—or Columbus, as he is more usually called —thought that he had found India. Never, in the fourteen years that remained to him after he had made history's most important voyage, did he fully realize that he had discovered, not the Indies, but a world unknown to geographers, a new world. He had landed on an island of the Caribbean, generally thought to be Watling Island, in the Bahamas. "The lands," he wrote, "are all most beautiful . . . and full of trees of a thousand kinds, so lofty that they seem to reach the sky. And some of them were in flower, some in fruit, some in another stage according to their kind. And the nightingale was singing, and other birds of a thousand sorts, in the month of November."

The islands were peopled. Columbus tells us: "The people of this island, and of all the others that I have found and seen . . . all go naked, men and women . . . they are artless and generous with what they have, to such a degree as no one would believe but he who had seen it." He described them as "very well made, with very handsome bodies, and very good countenances. Their hair is short and coarse, almost like the hairs of a horse's tail."

And, of course, he called them Indians. "As soon as I had landed on the first island that I encountered in that sea I had several Indians taken prisoner." *Quosdam Indos,* in the Latin original text: "several Indians."

Indians they have remained, and no one can alter

that now. The name is so firmly established that the real Indians, those of India, have to be referred to as "*East* Indians." Columbus not only committed a misnomer, he was also victimized by one, for the lands he discovered are called not Columbia but America—named for a later voyager, Amerigo Vespucci.

Indians, though not from India. And "red men," although not red. Such has been the fate of these people who lived in such splendid isolation for so long—their homeland taken from them, their very names inaccurate.

The people we must call Indians come in many colors, but never red. The color of their skins varies from tribe to tribe—for, as we shall see, there is no one standard type of Indian. Some are no darker than tawny-complexioned white men; others are olive-colored and swarthy; most are a pale brown, the color of fallen leaves in October. If anything, white men, with their pinkish skins, deserve the name of "red men" more than the Indians!

COLUMBUS, roaming the islands of the Caribbean, was unable to find the mainland he sought. He never reached North America at all; that remained for John Cabot to discover, in 1497. Cabot, sailing along the coast of frosty Newfoundland, may have encountered Indians of that region, who ornamented themselves with coats of red paint—the origin, maybe, of the "red man" myth.

The real immensity of the two new continents,

though, was not apparent to Columbus or Vespucci or Cabot or any of those bold adventurers at the turn of the sixteenth century. Not until hardy, gold-hungry Spaniards began trekking into the interior of the New World did the vastness come home vividly, did anyone gain any sense of the unimaginable distances of these virgin expanses.

In the hugeness of North America, man was insignificant. At the time Columbus landed, no more than a million Indians dwelt in what is today the continental United States. (A guess, of course; nobody was taking censuses in 1492. But it is an expert guess, and probably close to the truth.)

Only a million! In less than five hundred years, North America's population has multiplied two hundred fold. To the south, however, the Indian population was far greater. Perhaps as many as thirty million Indians dwelt in South and Central America when the white man came.

Suppose we could have surveyed our continent from a helicopter, in 1491. What would we have seen in the New World the year before the first white men came?

We would have seen great cities to the south. What is now Peru then contained the swarming millions of the Inca Empire, that tightly organized, almost communistic, state that spanned a twenty-five-hundred-mile stretch of South America. Modern Mexico then held two mighty civilized states: that of the blood-thirsty, pyramid-building Aztecs and, on the chalky plain of the Yucatan Peninsula, the sophisticated, calendar-devising Mayas. Elsewhere in the southern half of the hemisphere, the spying eye from above would have seen more primitive tribes, living in the steaming jungles of the Amazon basin, on the heights of the Andes, amid the bleakness of Patagonia.

In the North, we would have had to look more closely to see signs of human life. Four hundred thousand Indians dwelt in the eastern woodlands of North America, living in bark-covered wigwams, slipping through the silent forests with bow at the ready to bring down deer or lynx. They lived in widely scattered settlements, rarely remaining in the same place for long. When food supplies began to thin, these hunters and trappers and fisherfolk would move onward, endlessly roaming the woods of Canada, New England, and on down the coast.

The eye would not know it, but these simple hunters and fishers were far from savage, even though they had built nothing to compare with the stone cities and great temples of the Mayas, Aztecs, and Incas, their cousins far to the south. These eastern woodland people had complex languages, religions, customs. Some of them had actually formed political groups. Perhaps, even as Columbus' three ships moved westward, the Indians known as the Iroquois were beginning to form their League of the Iroquois of which we shall hear more later. It was an elaborate political unit which may have inspired the thinking of the white men who drew up the Constitution of the United States two centuries later.

Inland, above the valley of the sprawling Mississippi, the unseen observers would have detected more substantial signs of civilization. Here, in the fertile river land, lived the Temple Mound people. Influenced, perhaps, by the pyramid-building Aztecs, these Indians built pyramids of their own, out of earth instead of stone, and topped them with thatched temples where priests begged the favor of the gods.

Westward the land flattened out. Here was the Great Plains region, west of the Mississippi. The Sioux lived here—not the wild horsemen familiar to us in motion pictures, for in 1491 there were no horses in the Americas. Nor were these Sioux fighters, since the white man had not yet come to challenge them. They were peaceful farmers, even a little timid, who lived on the edges of the great grasslands and every few years moved a short distance west into the unknown. They numbered some hundred thousand.

Beyond these Sioux in their buffalo-skin tipis, there was an astonishing emptiness. No Indians dared to venture into the endless plains, and herds of buffalo, many thousands strong, pounded unmolested over the land.

As we continued on our westward journey, the terrain would have begun to change, the Southwest baking under a hot sun. Another hundred thousand Indians lived here. Some of them were city-dwellers, living in substantial stone skyscrapers. These Pueblo people, building with boulders or with mud brick, dwelt in cities covering ten to twelve acres and even more. Beyond

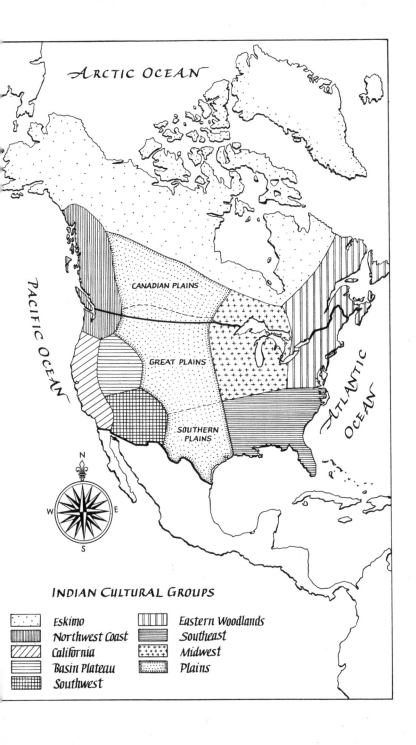

these peaceful cities, where the daily round of irrigation, crop-tending, and ceremonial dancing had been
going on for more than a thousand years, lived wilder
folk, nomadic Apache and Navaho who had come down
out of the north only a short time before. These unwanted intruders into the Southwest made life uncomfortable for the settled city dwellers.

Westward, then. One hundred thousand more Indians lived in the plateau and desert country of what
is now Nevada, Utah, Montana, and part of Canada.
These were hunting Indians; they did a little planting,
digging into the ground with sticks, but compared with
the Pueblo people or the Temple Mound Indians they
were little more than savages.

In the far Southwest, in California, giant trees
stabbed the skies—redwoods, growing in thick-packed
ranks, trees that were tall before the first pharaoh came
to rule in Egypt. At the feet of these monsters there were
more Indians, gentle ones, who lived by gathering wild
seeds. The climate was kind to them, and they faced
no challenges, nothing likely to goad them into developing a high order of civilization. The biggest problem these California Indians had was one of communi-
cation. Here in redwood country, every tiny tribe had
its own language. Hundreds of totally unrelated
tongues were spoken—more different languages than
in any other single region of the world. In this land of
Babel, a man could not travel more than a mile from
home without finding himself among speakers of a
strange lingo. But they did not travel much in warm,

sleepy California. Each tribe remained in its own snug harbor.

Northward up the coast, a different breed could be found. The Indians of the far Northwest were vigorous, highly developed people, builders of totem-poles and canoes, of elegantly decorated plank houses. These Indians in their colorful garb, these Klamath and Chinook and Tlingit and Kwakiutl, fished for their dinners, hauling salmon from the swift-flowing Columbia. The coast population numbered some two hundred thousand.

The remaining North Americans lived in the frozen Arctic: the Eskimo, people of the igloo and the kayak. Fascinating though they are, they fall outside the scope of our present field. By no stretch of the imagination can the Eskimo be called "red men"; they represent an independent group, distinctly separate from that vague, far-flung category we call "Indians."

Our imaginary journey has shown us an incredible diversity of peoples. Some lived in tents, some in apartment houses. Some were expert farmers, others had to hunt in order to eat, still others were content to pick up acorns from the ground. Some tribes had almost no political unity, others—as we shall see—had a quite elaborate structure. The number of tribes was enormous, perhaps as many as a thousand all told, some including only a dozen members, others many hundreds. At least six hundred languages were spoken in North America alone!

Temple builders, skyscraper builders, tipi builders,

wigwam builders—there was little similarity among the different regions. We late-comers lump all these people together and call them "Indians," but the more closely we look at them, the more apparent the differences become.

We have already mentioned the range in color—various shades of brown, from light to dark. What about the other physical characteristics of the Indian?

There is a standard Indian image. We used to see it on the one-cent coin, and then on the buffalo nickel: a stern, hawk-nosed man with jutting cheekbones. The stereotyped copper-colored, untalkative, feather-bedecked Indian of the motion pictures, tall and lean and menacing, represents only one of the many types of actual Indians.

There were lean Indians and stocky ones, and even some downright fat ones, like the Utes. There were tall Indians who approached six feet, and others who, on a tribal average, hardly made it above five feet. Some Indians were thin-lipped and hawk-nosed; others had flat noses and thick, almost Negroid lips. Although most Indians had coarse, straight black hair, wavy hair was not unknown. Generally, Indians had scanty facial hair, but those of the Pacific Northwest cultivated mustaches! And there were roundheaded Indians, longheaded Indians, broad-faced ones, narrow-faced ones.

Out of all this welter of physical characteristics, can any general Indian type emerge?

Despite the wide range of physiques, there are certain characteristics that Indians do have in common.

They are dark-haired, dark-eyed, and dark-skinned. (They are not "red"; neither are they "black," "white," or "yellow," but a distinct if variable color of their own.) They almost always have prominent cheekbones and faces that are large in proportion to their bodies. The upper incisors customarily have a shovel-shaped contour not found in Europeans. And there are certain other bodily features that enable anthropologists to group all the Indians together.

It must never be forgotten, though, that there is tremendous variety within this large category, "Indians." Only an underlying fabric of common features binds together the Indians of the pueblos and those of the eastern woodlands, those of the Pacific Northwest and those of Mexico. The differences are often seemingly greater than the points of similarity. Just why there should be so much variation among the original inhabitants of the Americas is a point that has caused considerable discussion, and we'll return to it in the next chapter.

With such a bewildering variety of physical types, local cultures, and languages, it becomes a challenging task to think of the Indians as a whole. The spectrum of their ways of life is so broad that it can be a little staggering at first look. With Indian cultures as different from one another as those of the Arabs and the Congolese, and with Indian languages as unrelated to one another as Turkish and Hebrew, how can anyone possibly begin to assort, classify, and understand these marvelously inventive people?

Anthropologists have tried to classify Indians according to geographical distribution. Generally, that is the method adopted in this book. But there are certain dangers that need to be mentioned. Indians, being human beings, and highly complicated ones at that, do not fit neatly into pigeonholes. Any scheme of classification involves some overlapping, and some inexactness.

It is not fair to say that there are as many schools of classification as there are anthropologists. Certainly, though, there is plenty of disagreement among the experts as to how many categories to employ. Some would say no more than half a dozen, others upward of twenty. Clearly, the Pueblo people are a different kind of Indian from the salmon fishers of British Columbia, and the Temple Mound folk different from them both. But grouping the more nomadic, less-advanced Indians is still a controversial matter, which is why you are likely to see the classification handled differently elsewhere.

Another way of arranging Indian categories is by language families. Indian languages are, as noted, numerous, and some of them are very intricate indeed. One tribe of California Indians had over one hundred thousand verb forms, for instance!

The first attempt at a linguistic classification was made in 1891, by J. W. Powell of the Bureau of American Ethnology. Powell's ideas were sound, but he did not have enough information to work with. He grouped the languages spoken north of Mexico into fifty-six separate stocks, embracing some five hundred different tongues. Later students, notably Edward Sapir, have simplified Powell's pioneering work, so that about half a dozen main stocks are recognized today—with some area of disagreement still remaining.

These stocks are designated by adding the suffix -*an* to tribal names. Whenever words like "Siouan" or "Iroquoian" crop up in the chapters ahead, it should be remembered that these refer to language families, not to tribes. Theoretically, all tribes belonging to one language family are related, and possibly they once were—but often, unrelated tribes would adopt the same language, giving rise to confusion when an attempt is made at classification.

The general linguistic stocks recognized today are:

1. *Algonquian.* The language family of many New England tribes, and also such Plains tribes as the Blackfoot and the Cheyenne.

2. *Athabascan.* The language family embracing many Northwest and Canadian tribes. The Apache and Navaho of the Southwest also speak Athabascan languages, indicating that they probably migrated from the North in fairly recent times.

3. *Iroquoian.* The language family of the Iroquois, the Cherokee, the Huron, and other tribes of the Northeast and upper Middle West.

4. *Muskhogean.* The Southeastern language family, including the Creek, the Seminole, the Choctaw, the Chickasaw, the Natchez, and others.

5. *Siouan.* The language family of the Dakota, the

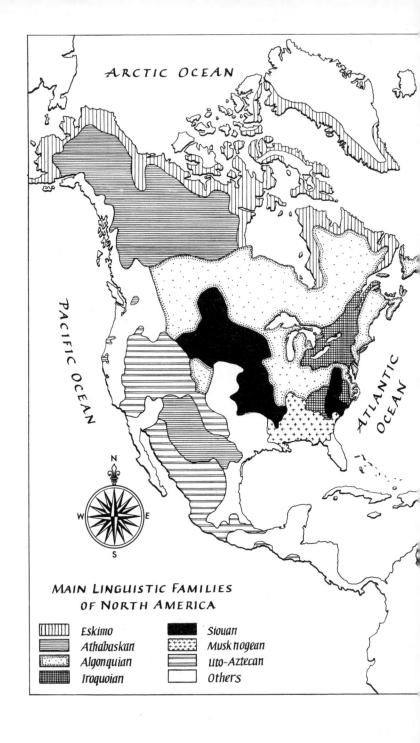

ARCTIC OCEAN

PACIFIC OCEAN

ATLANTIC OCEAN

MAIN LINGUISTIC FAMILIES
OF NORTH AMERICA

Eskimo		Siouan	
Athabaskan		Musk nogean	
Algonquian		Uto-Aztecan	
Iroquoian		Others	

Assiniboin, the Osage, the Teton, and other Plains Indians—and also some Eastern ones.

6. *Uto-Aztecan.* The language family of the various Pueblo Indians, such as the Hopi and the Zuni—related linguistically to the Aztecs of Mexico.

These six groups include most of the languages of the larger tribes, but by no means all the Indian languages. Completely outside the above groupings are the California languages, more than a hundred all told, and various other Northwestern and Southeastern languages which troublesomely refuse to fit into any sort of category except that of "miscellaneous."

A GREAT DEAL OF TIME and effort has gone into studying these fascinating Indians—though not nearly so much energy as early Americans expended in destroying them. On that starlit night in 1492, the million widely scattered Indians of North America, and the many millions south of the Rio Grande, could have had no inkling of the tragedy about to descend on them.

There had been visitors to their land before. Norsemen had come, about A.D. 1000, and had even planted short-lived colonies on American soil. There are legends of Chinese explorations even earlier. Columbus and Cabot and Vespucci did not really "discover" America; they simply rediscovered it.

After 1492, however, there was no stopping the inexorable conquest. A land of buffalo and cougar, of grizzly and wildcat, of pueblo and tipi, began to fill with white men who moved slowly but determinedly toward the Pacific. The forests fell. The wild life gave way. And the people we call the Indians yielded, not without stubborn and bloody resistance, until ultimately they became prisoners of war in their own country.

It is too late to mourn for past crimes. The domain of the red man has been taken over by the conquerors, and cities and freeways sprout in the old hunting grounds. After a fashion of atonement, the conqueror has studied the conquered. The Indians did not keep their own history, and we have done our best to re-create it for them.

Let us try to go back, then, to that time before 1492 —to that world that was, that world that is no more.

2

THIRTY THOUSAND
YEARS OF IMMIGRANTS

WE ARE ALL IMMIGRANTS OR THE CHILDREN OF IM-
migrants, we who call ourselves Americans. My father
came to the New World at the turn of this century. Your
ancestors may have crossed the Atlantic in George
Washington's time. Or, if you happen to be an Iroquois
or a Hopi, you can claim that your people have lived
here at least two thousand years.

Eventually, as one traces back the family tree of any
American (a term which includes the people of Latin
America, of course), one comes to a time when the
family emigrated from elsewhere. The Indians were
the first comers, but they, too, were immigrants once.

There is archaeological evidence to prove this—or,
more precisely, it is proved by an *absence* of evidence.
For decades, archaeologists have searched the Americas for some indication that man evolved here. No
proof has turned up: no fossils of manlike apes, no
relics of apelike men. The earliest skeletal remains of
men in the Americas do not differ significantly from
living species.

17

In other parts of the world, scientists have identified the skeletons of creatures who occupied a transitional place between apes and men. (No one seriously doubts, nowadays, that man evolved from primitive apelike animals, although only a generation ago a famous court trial was fought over just that point.) In Africa, a number of fossil almost-men have been found in strata estimated to be more than a million years old. From Java came the famous *Pithecanthropus erectus,* perhaps the oldest creature who deserves the name of "man." In Europe and elsewhere, many skeletons of Neanderthal man have been unearthed—a stoop-legged, big-headed creature who is recognizably human, yet not at all like the men of today.

None of these transitional types have come to light in the Americas, and there is good reason to think that they never will. The Western Hemisphere does not even have manlike apes such as the gorilla and orangutan; the most advanced primates of the New World are chattering monkeys. Most authorities today believe that man originated somewhere in Asia, or perhaps Africa, and gradually, over a period of half a million years or more, fanned out over the rest of the world.

So the Indians were once immigrants. And they came to the Americas fairly recently on the great scale of evolution. Just *how* recently is still a matter for hot debate, but only a few extremists would say that there were human beings in the Western Hemisphere any earlier than 30,000 B.C. At the opposite end are those anthropologists who believe the Indians arrived only three or four thousand years ago. Most experts, though, agree that the Americas certainly were populated by 15,000 B.C. Not very long ago, such dates were anybody's guess, but recent scientific developments make it possible to assign more positive dates to Indian prehistory. We'll return to the problem of dating in a moment.

Aside from the question of *when* the Indians came, men have long tried to solve the mystery of *where* they came from. Almost as soon as anyone knew that there was a Western Hemisphere, and that it was populated by men unlike Europeans or Asians, the learned speculation began.

One of the first theorists was a Spanish priest, José de Acosta, who in 1590 wrote, "It is not likely that there was another Noah's Ark, by the which men might be transported into the Indies, and much less any angel to carry the first man to this world, holding him by the hair of the head, like to the Prophet Habakkuk. . . . I conclude, then, that it is likely the first that came to the Indies was by shipwreck and tempest of weather."

Shipwreck, though, would not account for the presence of animals in the New World. Noah's Ark had come to rest in Asia; how had the beasts crossed into the Americas? Acosta put forth his guess: that somewhere to the north there was a part of America joined to Asia, or at least "not altogether severed and disjoined." This was, of course, long before any white men had explored northwest North America.

Others in those early days reinforced Acosta's idea.

It was commonly thought that the Indians must have crossed into the Americas from Asia. Not that there was any shortage of differing theories, naturally. There were those who claimed that the Americas had been populated by shipwrecked Phoenician mariners, or by refugees from the (mythical) lost continent of Atlantis, or even by a band of Welshmen, led across the sea by a Prince Madoc. In the nineteenth century a wealthy English peer, Lord Kingsborough, spent huge sums to prove that the Maya and the Aztec were descendants of the Ten Lost Tribes of Israel. The Church of Latter-Day Saints, or Mormons, still subscribes to this theory, but is almost alone in holding this belief today. The accepted view of most anthropologists is that old Acosta was right, back in 1590—that the Indians came across from Asia at a place where the New World and the Old were "not altogether severed and disjoined."

The place, it is generally felt, is Bering Strait, which today is a fifty-six-mile expanse of shallow water separating Alaska from Siberia. Bering Strait would not have presented any very great barrier for a seafaring folk. It is broken by two islands, the Diomedes, and the longest stretch of open water is only twenty-three miles. That would be no real challenge for even primitive canoes.

Furthermore, in winter Bering Strait freezes over. A bridge of ice is formed, over which men can—and do—cross from Asia to North America. There is little doubt that Indians came this way, perhaps by boat in summer, across the hard ice in winter.

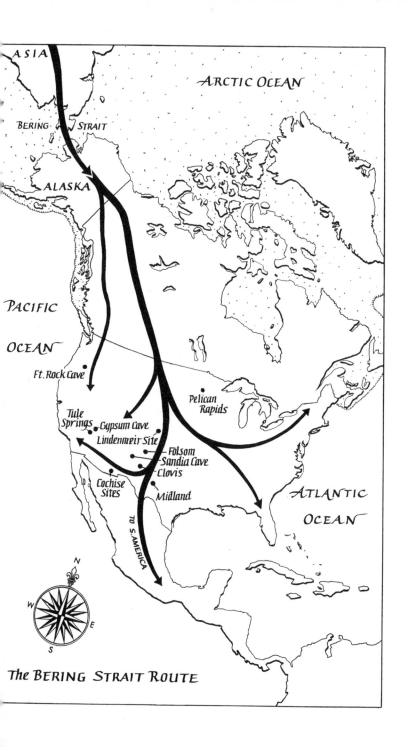

ASIA

ARCTIC OCEAN

BERING STRAIT

ALASKA

PACIFIC

OCEAN

Ft. Rock Cave

Tule Springs

Gypsum Cave

Lindenmeir Site

Folsom
Sandia Cave
Clovis

Cochise Sites

Midland

Pelican Rapids

ATLANTIC

OCEAN

TO S. AMERICA

N
W E
S

The BERING STRAIT ROUTE

It is even conceivable that the first immigrants to the New World crossed Bering Strait dry-footed, on land. This could have happened if, as many authorities believe, the great migration began during the last Ice Age.

Since the turn of this century, it has been established that four times in the world's recent history glaciers descended to cover much of the globe. The first of these four glaciations occurred perhaps half a million years ago, and the fourth some fifty to a hundred thousand years ago. (Guesses, again—but educated guesses, based on careful study of variations in solar heat.) Between these four widely spaced glaciations came periods of thousands of years of relative warmth.

The glacial eras have been given identifying names; the four European glaciations are called Günz, Mindel, Riss, and Würm, after the Alpine valleys where evidence of an Ice Age first was discovered. These correspond roughly to the four American glacial periods, which are called the Nebraskan, Kansan, Illinoian, and Wisconsin. The last of these, the Wisconsin Glaciation, is thought to have ended about 50,000 B.C., though it was many thousands of years later before the glaciers had withdrawn completely. (Some pessimists believe that we are only in an interglacial period now, and that a Fifth Ice Age may be on its way in another few thousand years. At the moment, however, mankind has more pressing problems with which to be concerned.)

There is very good reason to believe that man first entered the Americas during the last millennia of the Wisconsin Glaciation. If so, he could very well have crossed the Bering Strait on dry land. Those glaciers drew up an immense quantity of sea water, locking it in ice as the world froze. The level of the sea accordingly dropped several hundred feet. The weight of the glaciers contributed, too—depressing the continents, and causing a corresponding rise in the level of the sea bottom.

Now the Bering Strait is only one hundred eighty feet deep. Almost certainly, its bottom was above sea level during a great part of the Wisconsin Glaciation. For ten thousand years and more, a land bridge between the continents must have been open. After that, any immigrants would have had to cross by boat, or on the winter ice.

The evidence for this migration is not only geographic—the narrowness of Bering Strait—but genetic. For the Indians belong to the Mongoloid race.

This is not to say that the Indians are Chinese, or vice versa. The designation simply means that the Indians share certain body characteristics with such Asiatic peoples as the Chinese, the Japanese, the Mongols, and others.

The entire business of dividing mankind into races is as controversial and as difficult as any other attempt at putting people into pigeonholes. The boundaries between one race and the next are sometimes fluid, and anthropologists argue far into the night over certain borderline cases. Basically, there are three main stocks: the Caucasian, or European (white); the Negroid (black); and the Mongoloid (yellow). Each of these is subdivided in one way or another—the Caucasian stock is broad enough to take in not only the fair-skinned blond Scandinavians but also the brown-skinned Hindus; the other stocks are equally wide-ranging, and most of the argument rages over such hard-to-categorize peoples as the Polynesians, the native Australians, and the Ainu of northern Japan.

The American Indians are classified with the Mongoloids because they share such Mongoloid characteristics as prominent cheekbones, the shovel-shaped incisors, the generally broad-headed skull, the straight black hair, and the yellowish-brown skin. In some Indians— but by no means all—there are signs of the eye fold that creates the familiar Oriental "slant." And there are other highly specialized traits having to do with blood type, bone formation, and the like, which indicate a Mongoloid classification for the Indians.

So the evidence for a migration out of Asia across the Bering Strait becomes overwhelming. But it should not be thought that this was an organized trek, with thousands of people on the march, bearing all their belongings. At no time did the word circulate through Siberia: "It is time to emigrate to America."

What happened was probably a great deal more haphazard. Wandering bands of huntsmen, prowling through eastern Asia in search of food, crossed the Strait in groups of ten or twenty, perhaps. Families drifted across. The flow may have been two-way, with some of the wanderers returning to their homeland after a period of months or years in North America. Others kept on going toward the heartland of the New World.

It was presumably only a trickle, but a steady one. Maybe a hundred people a year crossed over at first, and possibly two or three or twenty years went by between the arrival of each group. The ice that had covered North America was retreating constantly, laying bare channels for the wanderers to use as they fanned out over two continents. The first red-skinned adventurers found an empty continent waiting for them —and as some of them continued southward, a second one! Food was theirs for the taking. Buffalo, elk, deer, bear—even such now-extinct beasts as the saber-toothed tiger, the woolly mammoth, the giant ground sloth—were the only inhabitants of the vast new territories.

For tens of thousands of years, the flow continued. The ice withdrew far to the north. The land bridge at Bering Strait was drowned by almost two hundred feet of water as the glaciers melted. Shore lines changed. The migration went on. There were Indians on the Atlantic shore now, Indians at the tip of South America, and Indians everywhere else. In the warm, obliging climate of South and Central America they flourished and began to build complex civilizations. These would reach their climaxes centuries later, about A.D. 1500, when the Aztec, the Inca, and the Maya had each attained their highest peaks—only to be chopped down by the cruel Spanish *conquistadores*. In the woodlands and plains of North America, no such civilizations arose. Far less numerous, the Indians of the North never equaled the accomplishments of the people of the Sun Kingdoms in the South.

The last to come, probably, were the Eskimos, who may have crossed from Asia less than two thousand years ago. Then the migration was complete. Fifteen centuries of isolation followed—and then brutal invasion from outside.

ALL THE FOREGOING is theory. In some places, it is bolstered with solid evidence; in others, it is pieced together in guesswork fashion. Since the late nineteenth century, archaeologists have toiled methodically to replace guesses with fact, and what we know today is more exact, more genuinely sound, than what we knew in 1930, or in 1910, or in 1890. Work goes on all the time and, for all we know, some startling new find may tomorrow change the face of American prehistory.

The best way to find out what happened in prehistory is to dig for the answers. Today, when a new building rises in a city, the one it replaces is usually demolished completely, rooted out without a trace to prove it ever existed. Other peoples were not always so efficient. It often suited them to erect a new dwelling right over the foundations of the old. Sometimes, layer after layer of occupation can be found—with the oldest at the bottom, of course. Thus, when Heinrich Schliemann made his successful excavation of Homer's Troy in the 1870's, he discovered seven cities, one atop the other—and later workers on the same site found that Schliemann's count erred on the conservative side! The task of the archaeologist, therefore, is very frequently one of patiently digging downward through a site, stripping away layer after layer of man's handiwork in search of the most ancient.

The archaeologists of North America have had some problems not encountered by the men who excavated Egypt and Troy and the cities of Mesopotamia. For one thing, the North American climate is a variable one, except in dry places like the Southwest. Rain and snow and wind destroy the relics of the past in a few years, while a dry climate like Egypt's preserves them almost forever. Then, too, the North American Indians left no written records, so there are no historical clues for archaeologists to go by. And many of the American tribes were fairly simple hunters and farmers, whose artifacts of hide and wood perished with them. Finally, there were few areas of heavy population concentration in Indian North America. Since no more than a million Indians ever occupied North America at any one time, finding their remains is something of a needle-in-a-haystack proposition.

Despite these challenges, the work has been done, and is still being done. Just as the maps of early geographers were filled with blank spaces labeled *Terra Incognita*—"Unknown Land"—so, too, has American prehistory been full of question marks, debatable points, wild guesses, and downright errors. These areas of misconception and lacking information are being cleared up steadily, though of course we can never hope to wrest from time's grasp *all* the secrets of yesterday.

One of the big problems in archaeology is dating. Even in Egypt and Mesopotamia, where there are historical records to aid the digger, chronology is a ticklish matter. In North America it seems all but impossible to arrive at any dates at all in the absence of documentation. Yet it is being done.

There are two ways of dating archaeological artifacts. One is *relative* dating: "This object is older than this one, but not as old as this other one." The other is *absolute* dating: "This object is 8,500 years old, give or take a century." Until recently, the best we could hope for was relative dating, but new technical methods are making possible an absolute time-scheme for North American prehistory.

Relative dating is a problematical and controversial business. It is done, first, by examining the artifacts found on any given site. Normally, the oldest objects will be closest to the bottom of the heap—just as at a junk yard. By careful digging, the archaeologist can establish a relative order of ages among, say, different types of pottery. These can then be cross-matched with pottery types from other sites.

Of the various methods for absolute dating, the best known is Carbon 14 dating, developed by Dr. Willard F. Libby in the late 1940's. It is based on the concept of radioactivity: the notion that certain elements are unstable and tend to break down over the course of time.

Carbon 14 is a radioactive element. It is an isotope— that is, a form chemically similar but structurally different—of normal, unradioactive Carbon 12. All living organisms, both plants and animals, are constantly absorbing Carbon 14 throughout their lives. Since it is radioactive, it is continually breaking down and vanishing, but in a living creature it is steadily replaced through new intake.

At the moment of death, the Carbon 14 intake stops. But the radioactive decay continues at a fixed rate, and this rate can be measured. Physicists measure radioactive decay in terms of "half life": the time in which half of any particular quantity of a radioactive element will disintegrate. Carbon 14's half life is known to be about 5,700 years. If an animal's thighbone contains one ounce of Carbon 14 at the day of the animal's death, half an ounce will be left after 5,700 years, a quarter of an ounce after 11,400 years, an eighth of an ounce after 22,800 years, and so on until the amount of Carbon 14 becomes vanishingly small.

Carbon 14 dating is done by measuring the amount of Carbon 14 in an object, and comparing it with the Carbon 14 content of living matter. An archaeological specimen surrenders a tiny piece, which is burned and then surveyed for radioactivity through a delicate and involved process. Naturally, only specimens that once were alive can be used, since pottery, stone tools, and other inorganic artifacts never contained any Carbon 14 in the first place. Bone—particularly charred bone—wood, hair, shells, antlers, all give fine results. Of course, there are certain drawbacks to the system. Sometimes buried material becomes contaminated with fresh Carbon 14 that distorts the evidence—or a specimen may lose some of its Carbon 14 through processes other than radioactive decay. For these reasons, Carbon 14 dates are always given with a margin of error, indicated by the "plus-or-minus" sign ($\pm$). If the sampled specimen is only a few hundred years old, the margin for error may be as little as a decade. Objects of greater antiquity are sometimes dated only within five thousand years or more. The absolute limit for Carbon 14 dating is about fifty thousand years, since beyond that point the disintegration of Carbon 14 is virtually total.

There was a good bit of controversy about Carbon 14 dating when it was first put forth. However, it is generally accepted today as the most accurate way of arriving at absolute dating for ancient artifacts. It has been possible to test the method against certain objects whose age was known through other means—as, for example, wood from Egyptian tombs. The Carbon 14 dates were so startlingly close to the accepted ages of the coffins that most of the doubters were convinced.

Another method of absolute dating is known as dendrochronology—tree-ring dating. It is only suitable for use in certain parts of the world, but in those parts it works very well indeed.

In the early years of this century, an astronomer named A. E. Douglass was making a study of the effect of sunspot cycles on the growth of trees. Each year, as a tree grows, it adds a new ring of wood around its heart. In a dry year, it adds a narrow, dark-colored ring; in a year of heavy rainfall, the growth ring is thick, and light in color.

Dr. Douglass began by studying the growth rings of the long-lived redwood trees of California. But these venerable trees were not suited for his purpose, since their rings proved difficult to read. In 1914, an archaeologist working in New Mexico suggested that he study the wood found in the prehistoric pueblos and cliff dwellings. It was spruce and ponderosa pine, both of which have clear annual rings.

The astronomer plunged into the task, and soon found himself involved with hundreds of bits of wood taken from many abandoned Indian dwellings. Gradually he began to work out a system of dating. By counting backward, listing the dry years and the wet ones, matching the patterns of rings from one sample to those of another, he succeeded in arriving at a relative chronology. At first, it was not possible to assign definite dates to the specimens, but he did work out what he called a "floating chronology," covering six hundred consecutive years. Through work of the most painstaking sort, he ultimately developed a chart of tree-ring patterns going back 1,229 years—from A.D. 1929 to A.D. 700. Further research has pushed this "tree-ring calendar" back as far as 59 B.C.

Archaeologists who work in the American Southwest today thus have a valuable dating tool at their disposal. If they can locate a fragment of pine, spruce, or fir from an ancient Indian dwelling, they can pin down its exact date simply by comparing its tree-ring pattern with Dr. Douglass' master chart. Interestingly, the dates achieved through dendrochronology check out when tested by Carbon 14 dating, and vice versa—one of the great vindications of both techniques.

Unfortunately, dendrochronology seems to work only with certain types of tree, and in certain climates. Attempts to extend the method to non-southern sites have not been very successful, though a student of Dr. Douglass' has managed to work out a tree-ring calendar for Alaska going back to A.D. 978. However, the method is valuable in its place, and perhaps the future will see its application in many parts of the world.

The field of archaeological chronology is a fascinating one, and deserves many chapters. Carbon 14 dating and dendrochronology are only two of a host of techniques used by archaeologists, but we cannot pause to discuss the others in detail. Let it simply be said that a vast amount of brilliant detective work has been carried out, most of it in the past forty years, and that when archaeologists assign dates to ancient objects, they do so on serious scientific evidence.

3

ANCIENT MEN IN
THE NEW WORLD

THERE IS A SHROUD OF MYSTERY SURROUNDING THE first twenty-five thousand years of man's career in the New World. We know—through Carbon 14 dating chiefly—that human beings were living in the Americas many thousands of years ago. On Santa Rosa Island off the California coast, the remains of dwarf mammoths have been found, their bones charred and separated as though they had been butchered for a prehistoric barbecue. The Carbon 14 date for these charred bones is about 27,000 B.C. And at Tule Springs, Nevada, split and burned bones have been dated at 26,000 B.C.

We have no real proof that the fires in which these mammoths burned were man-made. Some archaeologists still refuse to accept either the Santa Rosa or Tule Springs dates as valid. Regardless, the overwhelming burden of evidence is adding up to the almost certain presence of men in North America thirty thousand years ago. And, as we shall see, there is indisputable proof that humans were here at least as early as 10,000 B.C.

But we can trace back the Indian cultures that we know only some two thousand years at best. Before that, we have a number of question marks—and not, so far, any really coherent story of man's existence in this hemisphere.

The picture that we do have is formed largely by a number of "points." These are artifacts chipped from stone; they may have been arrowheads or they may have been spear points, but since there is no sure way of telling which, they are simply called "points." The different types of points have led to the identification of a number of varying early cultures, named, generally, for the place where the type of point first was found.

There is not much in the way of skeletal evidence to support the information the points give us. Intensive archaeological work over the past hundred years has turned up only about two dozen skeletons of early man in North America—a remarkably sparse gathering. Why so few? For one thing, the Americas were probably sparsely inhabited ten thousand years ago and earlier. Possibly only twenty or thirty thousand human beings dwelt in all of North and South America at any one time. In that case, it is not surprising that we should have found so few skeletal remains. Then, too, the primitive Americans may have practiced forms of burial that tended to destroy bones—such as exposing the bodies of the dead to the elements, or cremating them.

Whatever the reason, we have only a handful of old bones to show for early man in the New World. By and large, they are a troublesome bunch of bones, too—for what most of them show is that the Americans of 10,000 B.C. or so did not look much like Indians!

The few early skulls that we have are extremely longheaded and narrow. Most Indians, though, have round, broad skulls. Some, like the Indians of the Plains and the Northeast, are indeed longheaded, but their skulls do not very much resemble the few ancient ones that have been found. These old skulls have low foreheads and strong brow ridges, two features that are characteristic of man's earliest years. The scattered evidence leads archaeologists to think that the first Americans were quite different in appearance from the later Indians—that, in fact, the Indians we know came late to the New World.

All this is highly problematical. Not enough is known to make final judgments. We can only make guesses, and probably not very good ones. Early America still holds many secrets.

WHEN WE COME TO THE POINTS, though, we are on firmer ground. The most famous of the points, the Folsom point, served to end once and for all the argument over the antiquity of man in the Americas.

Until 1927, many respectable scientists insisted strongly that no human beings had lived in the Americas earlier than about two thousand years ago. The few strange, longheaded, big-browed skulls that had come to light were dismissed as irrelevant. Even the ancient flint tools—the axes and points—that had been found, were considered "recent" by the men who opposed the idea of the antiquity of American human beings.

In 1927, J. D. Figgins of the Denver Museum of Natural History was engaged in archaeological work near the town of Folsom, New Mexico. The year before, Figgins had found an interesting and unusual point at the Folsom site. It was about two inches long, made of a pinkish-brown stone called "chert." Down the center of each face, a single long narrow groove, or "fluting," had been carved. The outer edges of the point had been very delicately worked and ground. It was an attractive point, obviously the product of a skilled craftsman.

Figgins found the 1926 point embedded in the clay surrounding a bone from the skeleton of an extinct bison. Everyone agreed that that particular species of bison had been extinct for thousands of years. Figgins thought that his point proved that man had been alive and hunting bison with spears or arrows, perhaps ten thousand years ago.

No, the experts said. The point he had found was "intrusive"—that is, it came from a later time, and had somehow worked itself down to the level of the bison bones. Perhaps, they suggested, a burrowing rodent had buried it in the older strata.

Figgins dug again in 1927. This time he made an even more startling find: another point of the same type, this time lodged *between the ribs* of a bison!

He halted all work immediately and shot off telegrams to all the important archaeologists in the country, inviting them to come and see his discovery exactly as he had found it. Only three bothered to come: Dr.

Barnum Brown of the American Museum of Natural History, Dr. A. V. Kidder of Phillips Academy, and Dr. Frank H. H. Roberts, Jr., of the Smithsonian Institution. They came, they saw, and they were convinced. Intrusive? The work of a rodent? No. There lay the point, between the bison's ribs. Its evidence could no longer be argued away.

Further work at the site uncovered the remains of twenty-three bison altogether, and nineteen Folsom points. Significantly, most of the bison were lacking their tail bones. This was a good indication that the animals had been skinned for their hides. As Barnum Brown put it, "When you skin an animal, the tail goes with the hide." Figgins' find had settled one question. Man in America was at least as old as the extinct bison he had hunted—and everyone agreed the bison had died out ten thousand years ago.

Since 1927, Folsom points have turned up in many parts of North America—from Alaska to Georgia, in fact. Folsom Man as the maker of the points is now called, was a rover and a hunter. Clad in animal skins, armed with spears tipped with elegantly fashioned points (it is not thought that the bow and arrow were invented so early), he roamed the vast North American continent, preying on creatures who have been extinct a hundred centuries: bison and camel and mammoth and peccary.

Radiocarbon dating has backed up the original guess of Folsom Man's antiquity. The evidence at the various Folsom sites indicates that he flourished from about

eleven thousand to about nine thousand years ago. The
oldest carbon dating so far comes from Lindenmeir,
Colorado, where bits of charcoal were dated at an age of
$10,780 \pm 375$ years. (Remember that the Folsom points
themselves, being inorganic, cannot be dated through
Carbon 14. Only bone or wood at the Folsom sites can
be used.)

We have found Folsom Man's points, but not Folsom
Man himself. Not a single human skeleton has ever
been found that can be linked with the Folsom points.
This is not very surprising. As a wandering hunter,
Folsom Man probably simply left his dead where they
lay, or cremated them. "Under such circumstances," one
archaeologist has written, "it would be the merest
chance to come across a skeleton of Folsom Man anywhere in the enormous area of our Great Plains country.
It would be even more remarkable to recognize him as
such, unless he had a Folsom point in his hand or was
holding an elephant by the tail."

MANY OTHER TYPES OF ANCIENT POINTS have been
found in North America, each one indicating a separate
population of nomadic hunters. It is not likely that
the different points were the products of a single band
of men. When primitive man developed a way of doing something, he usually went on doing it that way,
without variation, for hundreds or thousands of years.
Folsom Man was one "tribe," with one tradition of
point-making. Different traditions were represented in
other areas.

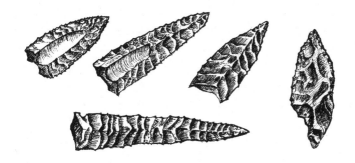

For example, there is the Eden point, first identified in Wyoming. This is a large, long point, magnificently carved. It does not have the central fluting of the Folsom point. Eden points are thought to be more than seven thousand years old. Another type is the Clovis point, from New Mexico—similar to Folsom, but larger and less carefully made. Yet another is the Plainview point, first found in Texas in 1945, associated with dismembered skeletons of mammoths and jaguar. It is also Folsom-like, but unfluted and chipped somewhat differently. All these various points argue for the existence of a number of bands of roving hunters in North America about ten thousand years ago.

And earlier?

For a decade, Folsom Man was the earliest-known inhabitant of North America. Then, in 1936, an archaeologist named Frank C. Hibben began to examine Sandia Cave, in New Mexico, which had been used by men for thousands of years.

Hibben found a layer of Pueblo Indian artifacts on the top level—broken pottery, fragments of baskets and sandals—all quite recent and not at all extraordinary. Below this level, the archaeologists came to a layer of travertine, a kind of limestone formed by water dripping from the cave roof. This layer, which was up to six inches thick, could have been deposited only at a time when New Mexico's climate was far rainier than it is today.

Hibben and his co-workers hammered away the travertine and were delighted to find in another layer, further signs of human occupancy of the cave. This new layer contained the shattered bones of bison, mammoth, camel, ground sloth, wolf, and other long-extinct types of animal—and some Folsom points! This showed that Sandia Cave had been occupied eight to ten thousand years ago. But the archaeologists did not quit there. A basic rule of archaeology is that one keeps digging until one can dig no more—until virgin, untouched soil or rock is reached.

They dug on. Clearing away the layer of Folsom Man, they uncovered a deposit of yellow ochre, a substance produced by fir and spruce trees under conditions of cold and moistness. The layer ranged in thickness from two inches to two feet, indicating a lengthy period of deposit. And beneath the ochre the excited diggers came upon another stratum of human occupation. They found, once again, bones of mammoth, camel, and bison. The bones had been cracked open for their marrow. Ash-filled fireplaces indicated the sites of ancient barbecue pits. The tools of prehistoric man lay scattered about: flint knives, and scrapers, and projectile points.

These points were not of the Folsom type. They were larger and more crudely made. Obviously they were much older than the Folsom points, since they had been found sealed off beneath the layer of yellow ochre. How much older? Possibly ten thousand years or more. Preliminary Carbon 14 tests on the Sandia Cave site seem to point to a date of about 20,000 B.C. At the moment, Sandia Man is the earliest-known maker of tools in the Americas. But who knows what further secrets the earth may hold?

As the situation stands today, we have projectile points of many different kinds, some rather odd human skulls, and a few heaps of charred animal bones from what may or may not have been the scenes of human feasts thousands of years ago. Can these random, scattered clues be pieced together to form some sort of picture of man's early career in the New World?

Perhaps. But we have to qualify everything by calling it not proven.

The story begins in the dim past—thirty thousand years ago, if we can believe the Carbon 14 datings from Santa Rosa Island, and possibly even earlier. A few wanderers out of Asia crossed into North America, perhaps over a land bridge, perhaps across frozen waters. These first-comers had long, narrow heads; thick, prominent eyebrows; and low foreheads.

They lived by hunting. They had already learned the art of shaping stone into sharp points, and of lashing these points to a piece of wood to form a spear. They lived off the big game of the North, the bison and the mammoth. They knew how to use fire, and cooked their meat. They wrapped themselves in the hides of animals.

These first emigrants did not yet know how to make pottery, though. Nor could they weave baskets, nor did they practice the arts. (So far as we know, at any rate. In 1959, a Mexican anthropologist named Juan Armenta made an important discovery which may cause us to revise some of our ideas about the artistic tendencies of the earliest Americans. What Dr. Armenta found, at a site near Puebla, Mexico, was a group of four fragments of mammoth bone, on which were engraved hunting scenes, serpents, mammoths, camels, and catlike figures. Not only are the designs done with remarkable artistic skill, but they may have been carved on fresh-killed animals' bones—some thirty thousand years ago!)

These early men fanned outward in a number of directions. It was not really a migration. At least, it did not seem that way to them. They might remain in one spot for several generations, perhaps a hundred years or more, so that to the tribe it would seem that "we have always lived here." And then, seeking better sources of game, they would move on. In the perspective of twenty thousand years or more, it looks like a purposeful migration. Actually it was simply an extended gradual roaming.

We have some idea of the routes the wanderers took. Even if they came during the last Ice Age—and this seems likely—certain paths were open to them as they came out of what is now Alaska. For several thousand years during the glacial period, an ice-free corridor hundreds of miles wide existed just east of the Rockies, from the Arctic down into the northern United States. Later, another pathway was available through the Alberta-Saskatchewan plains, east of the Rockies. A different route led from the northern coastal lowlands to the Mackenzie River, and then south along its valley, which was never glaciated.

Perhaps by 20,000 B.C., men had penetrated into what is now the United States, always moving in search of the game on which they preyed. The animals probably kept close to rivers, and so did the men who followed them.

One group of wanderers came down east of the Rockies and spread out, in little hunting bands, over the western United States. Some of them reached New Mexico, then cool and rainy, and one day held a feast in Sandia Cave, leaving their spear points behind to tell the tale of their presence to Dr. Frank Hibben, some twenty thousand years later. Others kept right on going, on into Mexico, then through Central America, and down South America's western coast clear to Patagonia.

However long it may have taken to cover the eleven thousand miles from Bering Strait to the Straits of Magellan, men were there by about 8000 B.C. At least, this is the Carbon 14 date from Fell's Cave, Chile, almost at the southern tip of South America, where longheaded human skulls and charred animal bones were found.

The early Americans were restless. They built no communities. They paused from time to time in their wanderings, but never long enough to leave a permanent impress at any one place. Their projectile points, widely scattered, mark their presence in many parts of the United States.

While one thrust of wanderers was moving southward through the Rocky Mountain region into Latin America, another band was moving eastward in slow stages. Possibly as early as 11,000 B.C. there were huntsmen east of the Mississippi, living in the Great Lakes region. They moved on into the eastern woodlands. Fluted points, somewhat similar to Folsom points, have been found in the East. One hundred of them were discovered at a single site in Massachusetts, which provided a radiocarbon date of about 7000 B.C. In Vermont, Pennsylvania, Michigan, and Ohio as well, these fluted points have turned up.

The year 10,000 B.C. must have seen man well established in North America. By then, craftsmanship had advanced to the level of the elegant Folsom points, the related Clovis type, and the rest. But it does not appear that there had been a very great change in the nature of man's life over the thousands of years since his first entry into North America. He was still a nomad. He still had no real culture. He fashioned a few beads and trinkets, perhaps, but his existence was still primitive.

About eight thousand years ago, things began to change.

The most significant thing that happened then was the dying out of the animals. The big mammals that had flourished in North America for hundreds of thousands of years became extinct with a suddenness and a finality that pose a major scientific puzzle. At once —geologically speaking—the mammoth and the mastodon, the camel and the horse, the saber-toothed cat and the dire wolf, the ground sloth and the great bison were snuffed out and went the way of the trilobite and the dinosaur.

Why? Why all at once? Why so swiftly?

Some say it was man himself who was the culprit:

rapidly multiplying, increasingly skillful with his spear
and perhaps by now with bow and arrow as well,
he slaughtered his own food supply to the point of no
return. But it seems hard to believe that a few hundred
thousand widely scattered huntsmen could have wiped
out an animal population that numbered many millions. We do know that most of North America under-
went sweeping climatic changes about eight thousand
years ago, moist regions becoming deserts, cold woodlands becoming pleasant forests. Maybe these changes
did the big mammals in. Man adapted, the mammoth
and mastodon succumbed.

Whatever the reason, the big game animals disappeared. The people of North America changed their
way of life as a result. New techniques, new methods
appeared. We do not know whether the new ways developed in North America, or whether they were
brought over by later waves of immigrants. Perhaps
Folsom Man and the other huntsmen, baffled by the
dying out of their quarry, vanished from the scene
themselves, and newcomers poured out of Asia to take
their place.

At any rate, there were changes. American man
passed from the hunting stage to the food-gathering
stage. He developed skills such as basketry, and implements like cooking vessels made of wood, bark, or skin;
also the bow, the spear-thrower, the harpoon. He domesticated the dog. He began to settle in semipermanent communities. Life took on a new richness and complexity. Now that the big game animals were gone;

man had to depend for food on lesser animals, and on fruits and berries gathered in the wild. New challenges brought new responses—and progress.

In Wisconsin, one group learned how to work copper. From it they made spear points, harpoon heads, awls, and many other articles. Until recently, this group, known as the Old Copper Culture, was thought to date only from A.D. 600 or A.D. 700. Even so, in 1947, an important textbook on Indians noted that "it is amazing to find a well-developed copper culture" so early. It became even more amazing a few years later, when radiocarbon tests showed that the Old Copper Culture had flourished between five thousand and seven thousand years ago!

Copper work was unusual, perhaps unique in North America so early. But another idea was starting to gain a firm foothold in other parts of the continent while the Old Copper Culture was fashioning its remarkable lances.

It was the idea of agriculture.

The transition from hunting to farming has a halfway house: the food-gathering stage. So far as we know today, man in the Americas did not start to become a food-gatherer until after the big animals had died away.

The archaeological proof of this assumption started to come to light in 1926, near the town of Cochise, in southern Arizona. Dr. Byron Cummings of the University of Arizona examined a site at Whitewater Creek, where school children had found animal bones and

chips of flint. Cummings spied a mammoth skull; bison, wolf, and horse bones; charcoal—and also something no other archaeologist in North America had yet found: grinding stones.

These were slabs of stone, hollowed in the center, against which seeds could be pounded with other stones —a primitive version of the mortar and pestle. Further work in the area provided a clear picture of that early seed-gathering community.

Once the entire region had been covered by a vast body of water, now gone. The archaeologists called it Lake Cochise. Ten or twelve thousand years ago, men lived along the shores of this lake. They did some hunting—the mammoth and bison and the other extinct animals still existed—but they were not very active hunters, a fact demonstrated by the total absence of projectile points in any of the Cochise sites so far. Their main source of food was vegetable.

Which is not to say that they were farmers. They did not *raise* vegetables, they simply gathered them, collecting seeds and roots, and using their grinding stones to pound them down into some sort of flour. As the old game animals died away, food-gathering became more important—and spread throughout the region.

Not too far away, in Bat Cave in New Mexico, archaeologists have found kernels of a primitive kind of corn. Radiocarbon tests provided an age of fifty-six hundred years for these kernels, which were not wild corn, but a cultivated species. The Bat Cave kernels indicate that the Lake Cochise seed-gathering culture had begun to give way, within a few thousand years, to a food-raising culture, another giant step forward.

Almost thirty thousand years had passed, if we can believe the radiocarbon evidence, since those first few longheaded, low-browed hunters had come across the Bering Strait. There had been steady progress, slow but sure, from hunting to food-gathering to food-raising. During these thousands of years, the gateway from Asia had remained open, of course, and new immigrants had entered the Americas in a continuous stream.

These later-comers were not of the same physical types as the first arrivals. Just what they looked like is the subject of hot scientific debate. The anthropologist Earnest A. Hooton, in 1930, demolished the idea that the Indians of the Americas were all of the same genetic type, after a study of many Indian skulls from New Mexico. He found traces of no less than seven different physical types in a single Pueblo community. Hooton put forth his conclusions in a paper called "Indians of Pecos Pueblos," in which he said, in part:

"Briefly, then, my present opinion as to the peopling of the American continent is as follows: At a rather remote period, probably soon after the last glacial retreat, there straggled into the New World from Asia by way of the Bering Strait groups of dolichocephals [longheaded people] in which were blended at least three strains: one very closely allied to the fundamental brunet European and African long-headed stock called 'Mediterranean;' another, a more primitive form with heavy brow-ridges, low broad face and wide nose . . . thirdly, an element certainly Negroid (not Negro).

"These people, already racially mixed, spread over the New World carrying with them a primitive fishing and hunting culture. Their coming must have preceded the occupation of eastern Asia by the present predominantly Mongoloid peoples, since the purer types of these dolichocephals do not show the characteristic Mongoloid features.

"At a somewhat later period there began to arrive in the New World groups of Mongoloids coming by the same route as their predecessors. . . . These later invaders were capable of higher cultural development than the early pioneers and were responsible for the development of agriculture and for the notable achievements of the New World civilization. In some places they may have driven out and supplanted the early long-heads, but often they seem to have interbred with them producing the multiple and varied types of the present American Indians—types which are Mongoloid to a varying extent, but never purely Mongoloid. Last of all came the Eskimo, a culturally primitive Mongoloid group. . . ."

Other anthropologists have questioned some features of Hooton's ideas, but the basic theory is generally accepted today. The Americas were a melting pot, a catchall for many wandering races coming out of Asia.

Thus there is no such thing as an American Indian "type." Indians fall into certain categories of common features, but they are by no means all similar to one another. Some Indians are longheaded, and probably are descended more purely from the earliest invaders of America than their roundheaded cousins. Some Indians have flat, bridgeless noses; others, hawklike beaks. Some are dark brown in color, others almost yellowish.

By the beginning of the Christian era, the influx of races was almost over. The Eskimos, who are not Indians, had reached their Arctic dwelling places, and after them few came across the Bering Strait. A pattern that had been fluid for thirty thousand years began to cohere.

Indians of different sorts lived in different parts of North America. They did not resemble one another very closely from one group to the next, nor did they all speak one language. The woodland hunters of the East were different in almost all ways from the farmers of the Southwest, and there were equally vast differences between the other types of Indians.

It is time, now, to look at these varying groups of Indians. We have come a long way, from Sandia Cave and Folsom Man down to the threshold of our own time. For most of our journey, we have been dealing in conjecture and hypothesis. We have been manipulating shadows. We know nothing of Folsom Man's religion, his customs, his way of life. We have nothing of his but a stone point, and we are free to draw what conclusions we may from that.

But now we enter a world of kaleidoscope complexity. A vast diversity awaits us, and we can do no more than scratch the surface. The best we can hope to do is to begin to explore the world of the Indian.

4

THE WOODLAND
HUNTERS

THEY ARE GONE NOW, BUT ONCE THEY WERE NUMBERED
in many thousands, and owned a world. It was the
woodland hunters' misfortune to be the easternmost
of the Indians, and so they fell first when the white
men crossed the sea.

They are the history-book Indians, the Indians the
Pilgrim Fathers met. We learn the names of some of
their famous men in school: Massasoit, chief of the
Wampanoags, who signed a treaty with the Pilgrims in
1621, saying sadly, "Englishmen, take that land, for
none is left to occupy it. The great Spirit . . . has swept
its people from the face of the earth." Squanto, who
taught the Pilgrims how to plant corn. Philip, the Narraganset chief who led a bloody last stand against the
newcomers. We know their names. But they are gone
from the woodlands, and the woodlands themselves
are mostly gone, too. The sprawling cities of the East
Coast cover the land that three centuries ago belonged
to the Indians.

The Indians the New England settlers met—and exterminated—were of Algonquian stock. Algonquian is one of the great language families of the Indians, and one of the most widespread. Once speakers of Algonquian tongues occupied all of eastern Canada, from Labrador to Hudson Bay. Two thrusts of Algonquian peoples came down out of the North, one moving along the Atlantic seaboard, the other streaming southward along the Mississippi Valley. Firmly wedged between these two Algonquian prongs lived Indians of a different language family—the Iroquoians.

We do not know when the Algonquians first took possession of their woodland territory in the East. They were longheaded Indians with high-bridged noses, and that has led some authorities to think that they were early arrivals, coming in the days of the mammoth and mastodon, as far back as eight or nine thousand years ago. Others disagree. Harold Gladwin, whose views on Indian migration are lively and controversial, thinks they were among the *last* to arrive. "They probably began to arrive sometime around 1000 B.C.," he writes, "and kept coming for 500 years or so."

Early or late? The authorities disagree, and harmony is unlikely.

The Algonquians were hunters, at least in the northern reaches of their territory. Down toward what is now Virginia, they depended more on farming for their food, but the typical Algonquians lived by the bow and arrow. Because they were hunters, they could not settle into communities, but had to roam in pursuit of the deer, elk, and caribou on which they fed. Thus they split up into many little tribes, and subdivided into hunting bands of a hundred or so each. About every six months, all the Algonquian tribes would come together for a grand general meeting, which they called a "powwow"—one of many Indian words that has passed into the white man's vocabulary.

As hunters, the Algonquians traveled light, unburdened by many possessions. Those of the North had the birch tree, from which they could make light canoes. The bark of the birch served them for many purposes: they made bowls, serving dishes, and trays out of it, since they did not have the art of making clay pottery, or even that of weaving baskets.

Bark and light poles also served the Algonquians for their homes. They lived in dwellings known as wigwams, easily erected, easily dismantled when the tribe moved on to a new hunting ground.

Wigwams came in three varieties. The most common sort was a domed type, round or slightly oval, about fifteen feet in diameter. The wigwam-builder would begin by setting sixteen or twenty long poles of birch or elm in the ground along the boundary of the wigwam area, each pole with its mate directly opposite it on the other side of the circle. The poles were placed two feet apart, but for four pairs set one foot apart. The Algonquian would bend the poles inward, lashing each facing pair together with strips of linden or cedar bark. Lengthwise and crosswise supports were added, and the domed framework was covered with sheets of birch bark, or with woven mats. A smoke hole was always left in the center of the roof, covered by a movable flap operated by a long pole. Normally the smoke hole was left open, since a fire burned constantly in a shallow pit below it. But when high winds came, the smoke hole could be partially closed; and it was closed altogether during rainstorms.

Within the wigwam the Algonquians made themselves comfortable on foot-high platforms of poles, lashed together and covered with woven bulrush mats. More mats and skins were piled on these beds and on the floor.

The second type of Algonquian dwelling was the conical wigwam, sometimes called the tipi. It was built on a framework of two sets of poles—an inside set of supports and an outer set. To build a tipi, an Algonquian would set up four poles at the corners of a square, seven to ten feet on a side. The poles leaned toward the center and were tied at their tops. Then other poles would be added to round the square into a circle, and hoops of flexible wood would be bound horizontally around all the poles for additional strength. Strips of birch bark covered this framework nearly to the top, where a smoke hole would be left.

A third kind of wigwam was the "extended conical," or *wigawassawigamig*, again built of leaning poles. Whereas the ordinary tipi was cone-shaped, the wigawassawigamig was shaped something like a book stood on its edges with spine uppermost. A ridgepole at the top, two or three yards long, was the "backbone" to

Algonquian domed wigwam; tipi in background

which the main poles were lashed. The Algonquians also
built much larger lodges for religious purposes, along
the lines of the domed wigwam, but as much as two
hundred feet long and thirty feet wide.

Since the Algonquians lived by hunting, their religious practices revolved to a great extent around the
relationship between the hunter and the hunted. To
the Algonquian way of thinking, the spirits of animals
were powerful. "You and I have the same mind and
spiritual strength," an Algonquian magic-maker might
say, addressing the spirits of the animal world.

It was necessary to kill animals to live. Yet the
hunted creatures had to be treated with respect. Algonquian shamans—"medicine men" in popular terms—
constantly had to make offerings to the world of the
animal spirits, begging their forgiveness for the harsh
necessity of taking their lives. Algonquians believed that
the slain animals would not be angry if only their
bones were treated with respect. Therefore, to protect
the village against the vengeance of the spirit world,
and also to insure a continued supply of game, Algonquians, like many other hunting peoples in North
America, paid exaggerated respect to the bones of the
creatures they killed. The bones of fish had to be
thrown back into the water. The bones of land animals
(at least the skulls) were hung up in special lodges,
and were made the object of prayers and burnt offerings of tobacco.

There was little community religion among the
Algonquians. Certain ceremonies brought the whole

village together at the lodge of the shaman, but mostly religion was an individual matter. The Algonquian hunter went out alone to face the perils of the woods, and his religion was a private thing, a matter between himself and the particular spirit he regarded as his protector.

The sensitive feelings of the hunted animals had to be remembered at all times. Wasting meat was considered an offense to the animals. So when a hunter had exceptionally good luck and killed more animals than he and his family could use, he would throw an Eat-It-All feast, inviting friends to come and gorge themselves on his kill. At such times, the tent openings were

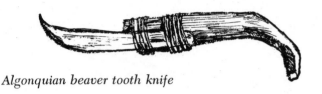

Algonquian beaver tooth knife

sealed, and no one was allowed to leave the feast until every scrap of meat had been eaten.

The hunting season for the nomads of the north woods ran from February to April, with another "open season" in the late fall. Each little tribe had its own loosely defined hunting grounds, and the men of the tribe journeyed there by canoe or toboggan, often going a great distance from the semipermanent village encampment. Deer was the chief game, but there were bear and moose and caribou also. The beaver was prized for its meat as well as for its fur. Porcupine, grouse, rabbit, squirrel, otter, and other small creatures were trapped to supplement the main diet.

The Indians preferred to hunt in winter because it was easier to track the animals then, and because the big game bogged down in the snowdrifts. To make their own movements easier, the Algonquians fashioned snowshoes out of rawhide thongs strapped across a frame of ash wood—an invention that is just one of our many legacies from the red man.

The Algonquians needed to be good stalkers. Their bows had a short range, only a little over one hundred feet, and for an accurate shot a hunter liked to get within sixty or seventy feet of his prey. Trapping and fishing called for ingenuity of a different sort; the Algonquians built elegant snares from flexible saplings, to which triggered nooses were attached. Let a roaming animal enter the noose to sniff the bait, and a moment later he would be dangling helplessly, high off the ground, as the bent-over sapling sprang back to an erect position! For fishing, the Algonquians used hooks of bone, baited with small fish. Salmon and seal were harpooned or speared. The Algonquians also knew how to make a poison from the jack-in-the-pulpit root that would kill fish without making them inedible, and they "harvested" great crops of fish by poisoning streams or lakes.

Except in the extreme northernmost end of their territory, the Algonquians were also a food-raising people. Among them, farming was a woman's job. The men helped, when they weren't away hunting, by clearing the fields and putting in the seed, but the women took care of the day-by-day work of tending and cultivating.

Corn was the chief crop all through the Northeast. Indian corn was colorful, each ear a flamboyant red and black as well as the familiar yellow. The Algonquians planted in April, fertilizing their cornfields with the little fish known as alewives, which swarmed in the New England streams. The white farmers that came to take over New England in the seventeenth century took over the Algonquian farming methods, too —and recipes for such Indian favorites as succotash, hominy, and corn pone.

All summer long, the women tended their fields, "hilling up" the corn to strengthen the roots, diligently plying their hoes of bone to keep the ground broken. Another Algonquian crop was wild rice, common all over the East then, today considered an expensive treat for gourmets. Sugar was made from syrup tapped from maple trees; sugar cane was unknown.

When they weren't in the fields, the Algonquian women were busy with their needles or with their fingers. Mats for the wigwam had to be woven; baskets and fish nets needed to be fashioned. Clothing was made of deer hide, tanned and scraped and sewed with awl and thong. Children wore nothing but moccasins except in winter. The men of the tribe were content with a single strip of leather around the waist, but the women wore knee-length skirts and loose, poncho-like leather blouses. When an Algonquian man or woman had to work in fields thick with thorns or brambles, knee-high leather leggings were put on. Soft buckskin or moose-hide moccasins were universally worn. In the winters, which were harsh all through Algonquian country, robes made of hides were worn by all.

Those feather headdresses worn by all Hollywood Indians were unknown in the Northeast. The Algonquian men went without such ornamentation. Most of them shaved their heads, pulling the hairs out with tweezers made of mussel shell and leaving only a strip of hair down the middle of the scalp. This "roach cut" was short except at the crown, where the men usually let one lock grow long. A particularly celebrated Indian, who had distinguished himself in battle, might allow himself the luxury of wearing a single feather in his hair.

Algonquian clothing was decorated with porcupine quills—softened, dyed, and flattened. The quill ornamentation often was highly intricate and unusually attractive. A more famous kind of Algonquian decoration was wampum—originally made from shells, and later, after the coming of the white man, from tiny beads worked with steel tools bought from Europeans.

Wampum beads were used, at first, as ornaments for chiefs. Later—especially when the European tools made its manufacture easier—it also decorated the buckskin skirts of most Algonquian women. And it was woven into belts which almost took on the character of money. Wampum belts were used as ransom for captives, as tribute to stronger tribes, as payment to the shamans, and as a "written" record of public treaties. When the white men began to make contracts with the Indians in the seventeenth century, wampum belts of great intricacy solemnized the treaties.

The Algonquians of Canada and the Maine woods had little political organization. Farther to the south,

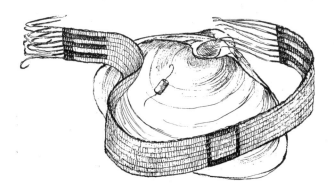

Wampum belt and clam shell: Algonquian "money"

through New England and along the coast down to Virginia, the Algonquians were organized into small confederacies. For the most part, these were informal and short-lived unions. Unlike their neighbors, the Iroquois, the Algonquians had little taste for elaborate political structures.

It was the tendency to divide up into tribes and subtribes that weakened the Algonquians when the Europeans came to colonize their territory. We read of a confusion and a profusion of tribes in the East —the Narrangansets, the Pequots, Mohicans, Wepawaugs, Naugatucks, Peconics, Penobscots, Massachusetts, Delawares, Wappingers, Powhatans, Pamunkeys, and dozens more. Although there were ties of blood and of language between these Algonquian tribes, local rivalries ran high, and they were easily divided and wiped out by the invaders from across the sea. Disease helped, too. The white men brought strange diseases with them to the New World, and the Indians, having no immunity, died of illnesses like measles and smallpox, which they had never known before. One epidemic early in the seventeenth century wiped out the Indians along the Massachusetts shore from Penobscot to Narraganset Bay, and this led pious old Cotton Mather to comment smugly: "The woods were almost cleared of those pernicious creatures, to make room for a better growth."

From Maine to Virginia, the Algonquians did form some political units. Those that we know about, of course, were active in the early seventeenth century.

What happened in Algonquian history before 1600 will forever remain unknown to us, since the Algonquians left no written chronicles. And by the end of the seventeenth century, they were so shattered and decimated that political organization was out of the question for them.

Quite probably, the pattern that the white men found in the 1600's had endured for at least several hundred years: small confederations built around the personality of one powerful chief, or sagamore.

In some of the confederations the sagamore's powers were limited, and he was hardly more than "first among equals." In others, though, the sagamore was something of an absolute monarch. One such ruler was Powhatan, head of the Powhatan Confederacy—known to us because of the story of his romantic daughter, Pocahontas.

Powhatan's "real" name was Wahunsonacaw—but that was simply his private name. As Powhatan of the Powhatans, he built an Algonquian confederation in the latter part of the sixteenth century which, at its highest point, embraced more than two hundred villages, each paying him tribute of skins, corn, and fresh-water pearls. Powhatan ruled his confederacy with a strength that seems to have been unique among the Algonquians. (Remember how he highhandedly ordered the execution of Captain John Smith—only to spare him, according to the pretty tale, at Pocahontas' tearful request.)

The Powhatan Confederacy did not long survive

Powhatan's death. In 1607, English settlers came to
Virginia, center of the Powhatans, and eleven years
later Powhatan himself died. Although the old sagamore's relations with the English had been relatively
good, his successor, Opechancanough, rashly attempted
to wipe out the white colony. A savage raid by the
Powhatans in 1622 took three hundred and fifty European lives and touched off a war to the death between
white man and Indian in Virginia. By the middle of the
seventeenth century, all that remained of the once-
mighty Powhatans was a poverty-stricken band of
survivors.

The archaeological evidence seems to indicate other
Algonquian confederacies up and down the Atlantic
coast—the Abenaki in Maine, the Delawares along the
Middle Atlantic region (the Dutch bought Manhattan
Island from a tribe of the Delaware Confederacy called
the Canarsies), the Wappingers in New York, and many
others.

Algonquians were warriors as well as hunters. War
was both a sport and a necessity for them. One way of
proving maturity, of becoming a man, was to take part
in a commando raid on another tribe. Algonquian war
parties would steal through the forest, carrying bow
and arrow, scalping knife, and tomahawk, for a lightning swoop on some tribe of enemies. This sort of warfare had an almost religious meaning to them.

Then there was the harsher warfare caused by the
need to defend one's hunting grounds. The various
Algonquian tribes not only constantly jostled one an-

other, but also had to fend off the alien tribes on their borders, particularly the fierce Iroquois just to the west, whose attacks were a constant feature of Algonquian life, except in the more isolated regions where they could live in peace.

And then, in the seventeenth century, came a new kind of war, a war to the death against the strangers with white skins. The Algonquians did not stand a chance. Divided among themselves, fighting their own civil wars even as they tried to drive out the Europeans, they fell by the thousands. A century of bloody war practically exterminated them.

Some stragglers remain, but they are no longer pure-blooded Indians. There are a few Pequots and Mohicans, a handful of Penobscots and Pamunkeys. But the Algonquians of the forests, the long-nosed hunters, who once loped through the woodlands of New England and Pennsylvania and Delaware and Virginia, are gone.

They have left reminders of their presence, though. Snowshoes and toboggans, moccasins, canoes, and many other Algonquian possessions have passed into the civilization of the invaders. And a hundred names on the map—Massachusetts, Connecticut, Delaware, Canarsie, Rockaway, Narraganset, Penobscot, Potomac, Manhasset, and more—mark the passing of the Algonquians from their hunting grounds.

5

PEOPLE OF
THE LONGHOUSE

BETWEEN THE ALGONQUIANS OF THE ATLANTIC COAST and those of the Great Lakes lived Indians of another language family, Indians of a different way of life. They called themselves *Hodenosaunee*—"People of the Long-house," but their Algonquian neighbors had a less complimentary name for them, *Irinakoiw*—"Real Snakes" —which the French turned into Iroquois.

The Iroquois were the five most important nations of the Iroquoian language-group. Iroquoian tribes (not the Iroquois) were living around Lake Erie and Lake Ontario two or three centuries before Columbus' day. Later, they began to filter eastward into what is now Central New York. We think that the Iroquoians originally came up out of the South, since their language is related to the Indian languages of the Gulf States and Mississippi Valley.

By the year 1350, perhaps, the Iroquois were firmly established in New York, from the Genesee River to Lake Champlain, having driven a wedge between the

Algonquians of the Great Lakes region and those of the eastern woodlands. From west to east, the Iroquois tribes were the Seneca, the Cayuga, the Onondaga, the Oneida, and the Mohawk. These five tribes later formed the League of the Iroquois, one of the most interesting political concepts ever created by Indians of North America, and one which may have helped to shape the Constitution of the United States.

Surrounding the lands of the Five Nations were tribes related by language and custom, whom we call Iroquoian to distinguish them from the Iroquois proper of the Five Nations. These Iroquoian tribes included the Huron to the north, a confederacy of four wealthy tribes; the Erie to the southwest; the Tobacco Nation and the Neutral Confederacy to the west; and the Susquehanna to the south. The Iroquois of the Five Nations were constantly in a state of war with most of these Iroquoian tribes, as well as with their Algonquian neighbors. In fact, according to the Iroquois themselves, they were generally at war even with each other in the days before the League came into being.

The League was created, it seems, about the time Columbus was cruising among the lush islands of the Caribbean. Legend tells us that two great Iroquois heroes founded it: Deganawidah, son of a virgin whose face was "doubly pure and spotless," and his councillor Hiawatha (not to be confused with another Hiawatha of Longfellow's poem). Deganawidah had the *orenda*, the inner spiritual power of genius. Hiawatha was his speechmaker. The relationship reminds one of that of

Moses and Aaron in the Old Testament; it was Moses who conferred on the mountaintops with the Lord, while Aaron spoke to the people on behalf of his tongue-tied brother.

After Deganawidah had conceived the idea of the League of the Iroquois, Hiawatha paddled his white canoe from tribe to tribe, persuading them to consider the plan. The last to agree was the Onondaga, whose chief, fierce Atatarho, insisted that his tribe must have the chairmanship of the council.

The representatives of the five Iroquois tribes came together for what can be called a "constitutional convention" that lasted many days in summer. Finally they hammered out a code that began, "I, Deganawidah, and the Confederate Chiefs, now uproot the tallest pine tree, and into the cavity thereby made we cast all weapons of war. Into the depths of the earth, deep down into the underearth currents of water flowing to unknown regions, we cast all weapons of strife. We bury them from sight and we plant again the tree. Thus shall the Great Peace be established."

Fifty Iroquois chiefs sat on the council of the League —fourteen Onondaga, ten Cayuga, nine Mohawk, nine Oneida, and eight Seneca. Each tribe had one vote at the League's annual summer meetings, which were held in Onondaga country. The League of the Iroquois functioned something like the United Nations, in that it only dealt with matters of "international" concern. Each tribe continued to manage its own internal affairs, though when a quarrel became too knotty to solve the League might be called in as an arbitrator.

In the deliberations of the League, each tribe in turn discussed a course of action—always the Mohawk first, then the Seneca, Oneida, and Cayuga. The Onondaga chiefs, serving as moderators or "Firekeepers," did not vote. All decisions had to be unanimous, and discussion would continue, led by the Onondagas, until every tribe agreed.

The fifty chiefs who made up the council of the League were known as sachems—an Algonquian word, oddly, not Iroquoian. Fifty noble families were given the right to name the sachems, and when one sachem died, the women of his family would name his successor. The new sachem would have to be confirmed by vote of his own tribe and then by the whole body of chiefs. Besides these hereditary chiefs, the Iroquois had a number of "Pine Tree Chiefs," chosen on the basis of merit, not birth, who also had the right to speak at the councils of the League.

The resemblances to the legislature of the United States are obvious. Chiefs were elected to the council in proportion to the size of their tribes, as are members of the House of Representatives. Yet each tribe had an equal vote, just as each state does in our Senate. A "Firekeeper," who did not vote, presided over the deliberations, as the Vice-President does over the Senate. And there were essentially two "houses" to the Iroquois "legislature"—the hereditary sachems, and the popularly elected Pine Tree Chiefs. This is very much like the system drawn up by the founders of the

United States, who planned a Senate elected by the State legislatures and a House of Representatives chosen directly by the people. (United States Senators were not elected by direct popular vote until 1913.)

Did the framers of our Constitution draw some of their ideas from the League of the Iroquois? We cannot be certain. But beyond doubt the workings of the League were well known to the men of the Constitutional Convention, and it seems very likely that they borrowed some ideas from this unique and extraordinary woodland confederation.

THE IROQUOIS were far more complicated in many ways than their Algonquian neighbors, who were rather simple hunting and farming folk. As with the Algonquians, the Iroquois men hunted and the women farmed, and they carried out both activities in ways not very different from the Algonquians.

But where the Algonquians were loosely organized and seminomadic, the Iroquois were settled and conservative—a race of farmers and villagers, not wandering hunters. They built good-sized villages surrounded by sturdy wooden stockades, inside of which each clan lived in its own dwelling.

Iroquois dwellings are known as "longhouses"— hence the Iroquois' name for themselves, "People of the Longhouse"—and are quite different from the flimsy wigwams of the Algonquians. An Iroquois longhouse was constructed out of stout poles ten feet high, set vertically about every four feet. Rafters bent into a pointed arch were lashed to the tops of these poles, and the roof was covered with slabs of elm bark. A longhouse was usually fifty to a hundred feet long, twenty feet wide.

Within, all was dark and windowless. Fireplaces were spotted at regular intervals down the middle of the earthen floor. As many as a dozen families might share a single longhouse, living in an arrangement something like that of a Pullman car, with semiprivate compartments along the walls of the house. Each two families shared a fireplace on the hearth between their facing compartments. Holes in the roof permitted the smoke to escape eventually, but the atmosphere inside a longhouse was always murky and unpleasant to those

not raised in one from birth. One had to keep low, since the smoke tended to collect about six feet off the ground. Longhouse dwellers sat or lay down whenever they were inside.

The longhouse, despite its inconveniences, was sturdy and comfortable in its fashion, and many Iroquois today live in modern versions of it. The longhouse contained not only living quarters but storage space for firewood, clothing, tools, weapons, and preserved food.

The Iroquois were not outstanding craftsmen. They had pottery of a sort, and made other utensils out of elm bark, but they did not excel in such arts, except in that of woodcarving. They smoked clay pipes, made by molding the stems around twigs that burned away when the pipe was fired in the kilns. These little pipes were often ornamented with scratched lines or the faces of animals, but they had little of the grace and vigor of pipes made by other Indians.

Iroquois energy seemed to go not into the crafts but into political and religious activities. Iroquois government is a good example of matriarchy: the women held the upper hand. As we shall see, women often had unusual importance in the Indian scheme of things, with property rights and political power not found among the European nations until quite recent times.

The Iroquois women owned the land and houses, and title passed along the feminine line of descent. When a man married, he went away to live in the longhouse of his wife. If he had daughters, they would remain in that longhouse, and would eventually inherit

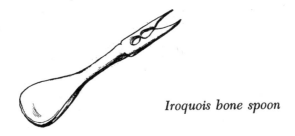

Iroquois bone spoon

the property and power of their mother. Every long-house was inhabited by several generations of women—an old grandmother, her daughters, and *their* daughters—and the husbands of the daughters. A man might take several wives if he could support them, but they all had to come from the same longhouse, since he obviously couldn't live in several places at once.

The Iroquois were divided into clans—large family groups tracing common descent. Originally there were only two clans, the Deer and the Wolf. Members of the Wolf Clan had to marry Deer; Deer could only marry Wolf. As time passed, these clans divided into others: the Wolf into Beaver, Bear, and Turtle; the Deer into Snipe, Heron, and Hawk. Each of the new clans remained associated with the original clan from which it had sprung, and so two groups of four clans apiece developed. Anthropologists call such groupings of clans "moieties."

In the days after the dividing of the clans, an Iroquois had to marry not only into another clan, but into a clan of the opposite moiety. A Snipe, for instance, could marry a Wolf, Beaver, Bear, or Turtle, but not a Heron, Hawk, or Deer. When a man married, he did not become a member of his wife's clan. However, any children of the marriage automatically entered their mother's clan, and were given a name belonging to that clan.

This arrangement, so different from our system of having the wife take the husband's name and leave her own family, gave rise to attitudes we may find hard to understand. A father, since he was not a member of his children's clan, was not regarded as a real relative. In old age, he could not count on being aided by his children. "Let him go to his own clan," a son might say. In the eyes of a boy, the real masculine head of the family was his mother's brother. This uncle trained his nephews in everything a boy should know. The sons of a sachem were not in line to succeed him at the League Council, but his brothers and nephews were. A man's mother-in-law was a person of such importance in his life that rather than offend her in any way he simply kept away from her, and did not speak to her except when absolutely necessary.

As mentioned above, the women of the family had the right to name the sachems of the League. They could also remove sachems if they were displeased by their performance in office. If a sachem were unsatisfactory, the women who had nominated him would give him three warnings. Failing to mend his ways, the sachem would be visited by the women, who would "remove his horns," taking away the badge of his office. Thus, although the women did not rule in person, they controlled the real political power in their immediate family and in the League Council itself.

War was an important part of the Iroquois life. The chief road to glory for a young Iroquois brave was through battle. Usually, a young man would receive a "spirit dream," telling him to go off and prove his valor, and small groups of young warriors constantly went wandering into the territory of Iroquoian or Algonquian Indians to win their mark of valor.

The principal weapon of these Iroquois war parties was the ball-headed club that the Algonquians called "tomahawk." Tomahawks were carved from a single piece of hardwood, two feet long, with a ball five or six inches in diameter at one end. The tomahawks were often carved or painted, and to render them even deadlier than they already were, some Iroquois would add a knob of bone, stone, or metal at the ball-pointed end. (After the white man came, the design of the tomahawk changed. The Europeans sold iron axes to the Indians, who used them for splitting European

Iroquois tomahawk

skulls. The new tomahawk had an axe at one end and a pipe at the other.)

Surprise attack was the Iroquois way. "They approach like foxes, fight like lions, and disappear like birds," one European said of them. A familiar goal of Iroquois warfare was the taking of scalps, a grisly tradition they shared with the Algonquians to the east. Like the Algonquians, Iroquois braves wore the roach cut, or sometimes shaved their heads entirely—except for the scalp lock at the crown, which made taking the scalp easier. Scalping wasn't necessarily fatal, although not many victims survived it.

The Iroquois frequently took prisoners, especially those enemies who were strong and valorous. A prisoner of the Iroquois was required to run a gantlet when brought back to the Iroquois village; women and children would form two parallel lines and beat the prisoner with clubs and thorny branches as he ran by. If he bore himself nobly and fearlessly through this ordeal, he might become an Iroquois himself by adoption into the tribe, particularly if the tribe had suffered heavy losses of men in recent warfare. Otherwise, a prisoner might be made a slave. A captive who was less lucky was tortured to death by the Iroquois women, who would surround him, mocking him with words of scorn as they tormented him with knives and burning brands. It often took a day or two for the prisoner to die—and then, after he had succumbed, his captors feasted on his body.

Iroquois savagery in warfare was legendary and forms

an ugly counterpart to their admirable political intelligence. Of the Five Nations, the Mohawk were the fiercest (the name comes from an Algonquian word meaning "man-eaters") and the annals of the Jesuit fathers who lived in Mohawk territory during the seventeenth and eighteenth centuries are full of ghastly tales of horror. To the Iroquois themselves, the business of torturing and eating captives was a religious matter, not a criminal act. One Jesuit records this prayer of the Mohawk to Aireskoi, the spirit of war and hunting:

"Demon Aireskoi, we offer thee this victim whom we burn for thee, that thou mayest be filled with her flesh and render us ever anew victorious over our enemies."

When the Iroquois were not slaughtering their neighbors, they were trading with them. All summer long, Iroquois men traveled a regular trade route in elm-bark canoes. They traded dried corn to the Algonquians for arrowheads and canoes, so superior to their own. The Petun, on the St. Lawrence, exchanged their tobacco for Iroquois corn. From the Algonquians again, the Iroquois got wampum, which they used in many elaborate ways.

Wampum, to the Algonquians, was simply a kind of decorative bead, though later on it took more complicated values. Among the Iroquois, wampum played a far more important role. They wove the beads into complex patterns which recorded the details of treaties, laws, and ceremonials. It was not really a kind of writing, but was more a memory device; the patterns of the

blue and purple beads prodded the memory into recalling the details of the facts being recorded.

Iroquois religion, like that of most Indians, recognized a host of powerful spirits with which man could have contact through dreams. The Iroquois were unusual in that they recognized a battle between the forces of good and evil; they talked of the Master of Life, who had created the world, and his brother, who constantly schemed to upset the Master's plans. These beings— and the animal spirits—were all pervaded by *orenda*, the invisible, supernatural, spiritual force.

Among the Iroquois, certain men were infused with *orenda* and had spiritual powers. Hiawatha was one; Deganawidah was another. Some lesser mortals also had special power. These were the members of the False Face Society, a group of shamans who healed the sick.

The False Face Society members wore masks of wood, grotesque and bizarre, which are the most distinguished form of Iroquois art. These weird masks had to be carved on the trunk of a living tree, usually a basswood. A three-day ceremony propitiated the spirit of the tree, who was given offerings of tobacco while the carving proceeded. Only when the mask was complete was it cut off the tree. Painted red or black, the eyes ringed with metal, the features sharp and clear, a False Face mask was always a masterpiece of the woodcarver's art.

When an Iroquois fell ill, the False Face Society would come to him masked, sprinkling tobacco and chanting prayers to drive out the sickness-causing spirit. One such chant went like this, according to the French explorer La Salle:

> "Partake of this sacred tobacco,
> Oh mighty Shagodjoweh,
> You who live at the rim of the earth
> Who stand towering
> You who travel everywhere on the earth,
> Caring for the people.
>
> And you, too, whose faces are against the
>   trees in the forest
> Whom we call the company of faces,
> You also receive tobacco."

Six great festivals marked the Iroquois year: the Maple Festival, the Planting Festival, the Strawberry Festival, the Green Corn Festival, the Harvest Festival, and the New Year, or Dream Festival.

Of these, the Dream Festival, held at midwinter, about the beginning of our month of February, was the most important. It was a festival of renewal, of

scattering old fires and lighting new ones. It marked
the passing of the old year and the hoped-for return of
spring.

Idled by the heavy snows, Iroquois in February were
tense, bursting with suppressed energy. The seven days
of the Dream Festival served to release this torrent of
energy. The Festival began with the ceremonial stran-
gling of a white dog. The dog's body, decorated with
feathers and red paint, hung on a pole in the middle of
the village during most of the Festival.

The days of the Festival were marked with games
and dances, and also by rituals. Important officials
visited each house, stirring the fires to symbolize the
coming of spring. The False Face Societies held
meetings.

A central part of the Festival was the telling of

dreams. All year long, the Iroquois had been visited in dreams by spirits. At Festival time, those dreams were to be revealed to all. Messengers went forth, announcing, "Now the ceremony of the great riddle has begun . . . for the Holder of the Heavens has decreed that the ceremony should be performed on earth as in the sky world." Each matron brought forth those members of her family who had dreamed important dreams during the past year. The dreams were discussed and interpreted by the wisest members of the tribe. When the dreamer finally understood the meaning of his dream, he had to carry out whatever instruction the spirit had given him, regardless of risk or cost.

On the fifth day of the Festival, the body of the white dog was taken down and cremated in the center of the village. The dog was considered a messenger, carrying the homage of the Iroquois to the abode of the gods. Then began wild war dances and finally the Festival came to a close. The Iroquois settled down to await the end of winter and the time of the Maple Festival, when the sap would begin to run again.

WHEN THE WHITE MEN came into Iroquois country, early in the sixteenth century, the League of the Iroquois was perhaps a century old. The Five Nations had welded a solid alliance, and they showed a unified power that the Europeans quickly learned to respect. These were no scattered bands of hunters like the Algonquians. The Iroquois were a cunning, sophisticated, and well-organized people.

They quickly struck up trade relationships with the

newcomers. The Dutch settlers of New York, afraid of the Algonquians of the coast, gave arms to the westerly Iroquois, hoping that they would help wipe out the Algonquians. The Iroquois also became fur traders, selling beaver pelts to the Dutch and the French.

When the beaver of Iroquois country began to give out, in 1649, the Iroquois turned on their wealthy kinsmen, the Huron, and massacred them for their beaver. Then the Five Nations liquidated the other Iroquoian tribes—the Neutrals in 1651, the Erie in 1654, the Susquehanna in 1653. The remnants of these tribes were absorbed into the Five Nations.

Conflict between this ever-more-powerful Iroquois League and the French drove some Mohawks into Canada, where they still are. But the Iroquois continued to consolidate their position. They allied themselves with the English, who had replaced the Dutch. They welcomed, in 1713, their Tuscarora cousins from North Carolina, who had been driven out of their homeland by colonists, and the Five Nations became the Six Nations. The scattered survivors of such Algonquian tribes as the Delaware, Shawnee, and Nanticoke were taken into the Iroquois fold.

The French disappeared from the North American scene in the middle of the eighteenth century, and for a while the powerful Iroquois lived in harmony with the English settlers all around them. But in the struggle between the English and the Thirteen Colonies, the Iroquois made the mistake of choosing losers. The Mohawk, Seneca, Cayuga, and Onondaga fought on the

English side, while the Oneida and Tuscarora allied themselves with the Americans. For the first time in its history of more than two centuries the League had split up.

After the Revolutionary War, the new United States made treaties with the Iroquois tribes, treating them as sovereign nations. Many of these treaties were later conveniently ignored by the United States when it became necessary to take Iroquois land for power projects, but some continue in force. Unlike the Algonquians, who are virtually extinct, the Iroquois remain an important Indian group. They live on both sides of the U.S.-Canada boundary, and their numbers are considerable. Some have become Christians and live as though they were white men, while others follow the old ways.

The old League of the Iroquois still holds a spark of life. Some Iroquois still regard themselves as a separate nation, older than the United States, and they spurn American citizenship. In World War I, this faction of the Iroquois issued its own declaration of war against Germany, and sent a messenger in native costume to Washington with the proclamation.

There has never been a treaty of peace between Germany and the Iroquois. So today, although perhaps the Germans are unaware of it, they are still officially at war with the descendants of Deganawidah and Hiawatha.

6

THE MOUND BUILDERS

IN 1796, AN ENGLISH ASTRONOMER AND EXPLORER named Francis Baily, accompanying a party of settlers down the Ohio River, stopped to examine a group of great mounds at a place called Grave Creek. The mounds had already been opened by other visitors, and human bones and pottery removed. Baily wrote that the mounds must have been "built by a race of people more enlightened than the present Indians, and at some period of time very far distant; for the present Indians know nothing about their use, nor have they any tradition concerning them."

A few years earlier, another scientifically minded gentleman had examined similar mounds in Virginia. He was Thomas Jefferson, and he wrote a careful description of a mound, terming it the work of a "vanished race" he called the Mound Builders.

Since the time of Jefferson and Baily, these mounds, which are found throughout the Mississippi Valley and in many other parts of the eastern United States, have been the subject of constant study. They are perhaps the most fascinating archaeological relics in North America. We know today that the builders of the mounds, although "a vanished race," were Indians, but of a culture more complex than any that the white man encountered in the East.

There are thousands of the mounds. Some are low hillocks whose identity only an expert could recognize. Others are vast and imposing. The Cahokia Mound in Illinois, for example, occupies more space than the largest of the pyramids of Egypt. We cannot accurately refer to their builders as a single people, as Jefferson did. From what the archaeological evidence tells us, several different groups built the mounds, over a period of perhaps two thousand years.

In the northern Mississippi Valley, the mounds are hump-shaped, and rarely more than thirty feet high. Archaeologists excavating them found them to be burial sites. We call their builders the "Burial Mound Culture."

To the south, from St. Louis to the Gulf of Mexico, mounds of a different sort are found. These are elaborate earthen pyramids, usually square or rectangular, and flattened on top. Sometimes stairways or ramps lead up the sides of these pyramids. Mounds of this sort do not contain burials, but were rather the sites of wooden temples which rose on the flat summits. These pyramids are the work of what we call the "Temple Mound Culture."

Some of the mounds are built in the shape of animals —turtles, bear, snakes, foxes—and even human forms.

These are known as "effigy mounds." They are most commonly found in Wisconsin, although the most famous effigy mound is the Great Serpent Mound in Adams County, Ohio, an earthen snake 20 feet wide and a yard high that follows the curve of a river for 1,330 feet.

There are also mounds of geometrical pattern—octagons, circles, squares. They sometimes come in groups, as in the series of geometrical mounds covering an eleven-mile stretch in Louisiana. Some of these embankment mounds enclose mounds of the burial type.

The presence of all these mounds, over an area of many thousands of square miles, indicates a widespread urge to build. Indians in many places, over a long span of time, devoted themselves to heaping up earthworks so vast that they have survived through the centuries. Why did they build so energetically? And what became of the mound-building cultures, all gone before the white man came?

Archaeology has given us some of the answers.

We know today that the mound-building idea dates from about 1000 B.C., according to Carbon 14 tests on utensils and ornaments found in mounds in the upper Mississippi Valley. In what had been a region of simple woodland people—Ohio, Indiana, and Illinois today— a great mound-building surge began.

Where did the idea come from? Did outsiders introduce it? Or did it simply spring up spontaneously in the Mississippi Valley?

The experts agree that the concept must have come in from outside. Some say that immigrants from Asia brought it with them, since burial mounds have also been found in eastern and northern Siberia. But this theory does not seem to hold up under close examination. For one thing, the mounds of Ohio are *older* than those of Siberia. For another, why would mound-building people coming out of Asia go so far east before beginning to build?

The alternative theory is also controversial, but has won more support. It is that the mound builders of Ohio learned the idea from Mexico.

Mexico had long been the site of the most advanced Indian cultures of North and Central America. Thousands of years ago, Mexican Indians were building elaborate temples of stone, and mastering techniques of agriculture that did not reach North American Indians until centuries had passed. The temples of the Maya and the Toltec in Mexico bear startling similarities to the temple mounds of the north. The Mexicans built of stone, those to the north used earth, but the basic idea is the same. More than that, there were resemblances in costumes, agriculture, and art between the highly cultured Indians of Mexico and their cousins north of the Rio Grande.

We know that in later years the Maya were aware of the North American Indians. The *Popol Vuh,* a Mayan book, refers somewhat contemptuously to "the people of the wood," saying, "There are generations in the world, there are country people, whose faces we do not see, who have no homes, they only wander through the small and large woodlands. . . ."

We know that a thousand years ago there was a trade route leading from Maya country north to the Mississippi, and that trade goods strikingly similar to those of the Maya passed from tribe to tribe from the Gulf Coast to Wisconsin, and as far east as New York, as far west as Nebraska and Kansas.

Was there earlier influence as well? Did travelers from Mexico visit the Mississippi Valley three thousand years ago, bringing with them the idea of building mounds? It is likely, but as yet there is no real proof of contact between Mexico and the North at so early a date. Perhaps future archaeological work in the mound region will settle the question.

Wherever they got the idea from, the Indians of Ohio, Indiana, and Illinois built mounds. This earliest North American mound-building culture is called the "Adena Culture," from the place in Ohio where a characteristic mound was first found. Their mounds tended to be conical, and were used chiefly for burial purposes. The skeletons found in the Adena Culture mounds show that the Adena people were roundheaded, but frequently used a cradleboard to flatten the skulls of infants, for the sake of what they considered beauty. It is important to note that the Maya also practiced skull-flattening—another definite link between the two cultures.

These Adena people must have had a close-knit social organization, since the great mounds could only

Great Serpent Mound of Hopewell Culture

have been built through co-operation. One of their mounds is the largest conical mound in the United States: the Grave Creek Mound in Moundsville, West Virginia, which Baily examined in 1796. It is seventy feet high, and three hundred twenty feet thick at its base.

After the Adena people had been peacefully building their mounds for five or six hundred years, a new race of Indians came into the area. They were a longheaded people, whom we call the "Hopewell Culture," after the site in Ross County, Ohio, where they first were uncovered.

The Hopewells were mound builders also. They flour-

ished from 400 B.C. until perhaps A.D. 500, which means
that they were almost exactly contemporary with the
greatest era of Rome. These Hopewell people seem to
have absorbed their Adena predecessors, and a new and
vigorous culture sprang up.

The Hopewells built vast burial mounds and earth-
work embankments, often constructing them in groups
covering hundreds of acres. Naturally, no tractors or
bulldozers were used to build these great mounds, and
it must have taken months or even years of patient toil
to complete one. The work was done by carrying baskets or skin bags of earth up a slope. Archaeologists
have found the imprints of these bags atop some of the
mounds, the bags themselves having long since weathered away.

The Hopewell people developed a complicated religious system centering around their mounds. Of course,
we can never know anything of their way of thinking,
since they left no written records. But we can guess
from the tangible evidence that much of their philos-
ophy centered around death and the afterlife.

This inference is obvious from the elaborate nature of
the Hopewell burial mounds. Not everyone rated burial
in a mound, and probably only chiefs, priests, and other
important individuals were granted such an honor. A
Hopewell burial was a regal event. The dead man,
dressed in his most splendid finery, was placed atop a
platform of logs, or sometimes within a wooden tomb.
As in many other cultures throughout the world, the
dead were sent into the next world accompanied by

tools and ornaments that they might need there. One mound contained twenty gallons of pearls in a single grave. The Hopewells would surround the honored dead with jewelry of bone, shell, and stone; with breastplates and headdresses of copper; with ornaments cut from sheets of glittering mica. Sheets of mica would also often be wrapped around the body just before the earth was heaped over it.

Some of the Hopewell burial mounds contain only a single body. Others have a dozen or more, and one mound, the Seip Mound in Ohio, yielded ninety-nine burials! Some of the bodies at the Seip Mound had been cremated.

We can only guess, of course, but it seems, from some of these burial mounds, that when a great chief was buried, dozens of slaves were put to death and were buried with him to serve him in afterlife. This appears to be the best explanation for the mounds that contain a great many simply ornamented skeletons surrounding one lavishly bedecked body.

If this is really what the Hopewells did, they were following a pattern also known in Aztec Mexico and in many of the other advanced Indian cultures of Latin America. Slaves were commonly sacrificed there whenever a great person died. It is a burial custom found in many parts of the world. When the British archaeologist, Leonard Woolley, excavated the Mesopotamian city of Ur, where the patriarch Abraham is supposed to have dwelt, he discovered a royal tomb six thousand years old in which more than sixty slaves had been sacrificed for the burial of a king and his queen. So, too, among the Hopewells of A.D. 100!

The Hopewell people were skilled farmers. We know this not so much from evidence that has been found, as from what we can deduce. A culture that has time to build huge burial mounds is one that has an ample food supply, and that can come only through agriculture. Hunters and food-gatherers are so busy simply trying to feed themselves that they cannot afford the luxury of building mounds or of fashioning delicate jewelry. The Hopewells must have cultivated corn, beans, and squash, three crops, long raised in Mexico, which gradually filtered northward thousands of years ago.

They were also busy tradesmen. Archaeologists have found Hopewell goods in many parts of the country, as far west as the Rockies. Long before anyone in Europe thought of sailing to a new world, Hopewell merchants were active in North America, trading copper goods and exquisite stone pipes for seashells, mica, obsidian, and other materials that they used in their jewelry.

The picture we get of the Hopewells is of a well-organized, highly advanced culture. There is good reason to think that each area of Hopewell settlement was ruled by a powerful king, or by a group of priests. The Hopewells may have had a definite social structure, with nobles, commoners, and slaves. At the time they flourished, they were by all odds the most advanced Indian culture east of the Mississippi.

The Hopewells reached their peak about A.D. 500. After that, they gradually vanished from the scene for reasons which are not clear to us today. Just as they had replaced the Adena people, so did they give way to a new and more vigorous group of mound builders.

This new culture originated in the South, and centered along the Mississippi River from the Delta as far north as Cairo, Illinois. We call them the "Temple Mound people."

There can be no question at all of the relationship between the Temple Mound Culture and the city-building peoples of Mexico. Not only are the temple mounds themselves obvious copies of the stone temples of the Aztec and Maya, but the very arrangement of the mounds, in wide plazas, is a copy of the Mexican style, and the resemblances between Temple Mound artifacts and those of Mexico are too great to be mere coincidence. From A.D. 800 or so until the coming of the white man, there must have been regular contact between the Indians of the Mississippi Valley and those of Mexico.

The new style of mound building was quite different from the Hopewell brand. The Hopewells had built sprawling, round-topped mounds used either as fortifications or as burial sites. The newcomers' mounds were flat-topped and sharp in outline, and wooden temples rose at their summits. The earthen pyramids were frequently eighty to one hundred feet high, and covered acres of ground. Their sides rose steeply, "so upright," as a 1790 traveler put it, "that the cattle cannot get upon it to feed."

The Temple Mound Culture rapidly expanded out of

its southern point of origin until it had absorbed most of the old Hopewell sites, and by A.D. 1200 the Hopewell Culture seems to have been completely supplanted by its successor. The Temple Mound people made excellent jewelry and pottery, obviously influenced by the arts and crafts of Mexico. They were diligent farmers, and we have found their hoes, made of stone, shell, or the shoulder blades of animals.

Instead of burying their dead in mounds, the Temple Mound people built cemeteries surrounding the temples. Sometimes, true, they did use a mound for a burial, but it was never a vast mound such as the Hopewells built. Some important Temple Mounders were buried beneath the floors of the wooden temples atop the mounds.

The temples were built in clusters around a central plaza. Sometimes thirty or more temples would rise in the same village. Slanting ramps of logs, or wooden stairways, provided access to the temple at the summit, which was built of poles and thatch, decorated with daubs of clay. It appears that a ceremonial fire burned in the temple. There may have been human sacrifice.

The people themselves lived in simple wooden houses with thatched roofs, clustered around the temple mounds. A wooden stockade surrounded each village, and some towns were also protected by earthen embankments as in Hopewell days.

The Hopewells, and the Adena before them, had—like many Indian cultures—been fascinated by death. No doubt much of the Hopewell-Adena religious life revolved around the preparation for death and the rituals of burial. But neither of these early mound-building peoples carried their preoccupation with death to the length the Temple Mounders did.

About 1500, the Mississippi Valley was seized by a tremendous religious movement that we call the "Death Cult." The already extreme Temple Mound attitude toward death turned into a downright morbid one. A new type of art became widespread, grotesque and frightening, ornamented with figures of buzzards and snakes, of flying horned serpents, of skulls and weird faces. Just what the rituals of the Death Cult were, we can barely guess, but they must have been somber and dark, to match the kind of art the Death Cult era produced.

The Death Cult sprang up at a time when the Spanish *conquistadores* had already begun to make contact with the Indians of Mexico. Probably wild rumors of the newcomers had spread rapidly through the Temple Mound country, which was in such close contact with Mexico. Bearded strangers with white skins had come, riding huge beasts, carrying weapons that could kill like a thunderbolt. The terrified Indians must have begun to think that the end of the world was at hand. And they were right: for them, the coming of the white man *did* mean the end of the world.

The Death Cult marked the final burst of Temple Mound creativity. For a period of fifty or sixty years, the mound builders devoted themselves wholeheartedly to their new religion, and then suddenly—before the white man arrived—the whole mound-building culture came to an end. It disappeared without leaving any trace among the Indians who continued to inhabit the Mississippi Valley. As we shall see in the following chapter, there were certain survivals of the mound builders in parts of the southern United States, but the whole great culture seems to have vanished with chilling rapidity. The Death Cult era had been a last gasp, a stunning crescendo to the civilization that had inhabited the Mississippi Valley for more than twenty-five hundred years. And then—almost overnight, it would appear—nothing!

The riddle of the Temple Mound society still perplexes archaeologists. When the Spaniards ventured through the area, they saw the mound builders in their last days, but almost at once the entire culture was swept away, temples were allowed to fall into ruin, mounds were abandoned and became covered over with shrubbery.

Archaeologists have devoted much time and energy to exploring these mounds. They are the happy hunting grounds of the Eastern archaeologists, who find them the best source of information about the vanished red men of the region. Whereas the woodland Indians built little that was substantial, and so offer little to the archaeologist, the mounds are full of fascinating and revealing objects.

Unfortunately, the work of the archaeologists has not always been without obstacles. Some cities justifiably regard their mounds as local monuments, and will

not permit them to be dug up. Excavating archaeo-
logically entails a certain amount of destruction, obviously, and many of the most tempting mounds have
never been touched scientifically because of their importance as tourist attractions. Regrettable as this may
be so far as the pursuit of knowledge goes, it is certainly
easy to understand and to forgive.

A much more serious threat to our rediscovery of the
past comes from amateur archaeologists, or "pothunters," who want only to dig up mounds for their
own private profit. They attack irreplaceable archaeological sites with pick and shovel and do a horrifying
amount of damage, all for the sake of a few pottery
jars or bits of jewelry that can be sold at a handsome
price to private collectors.

When a real archaeologist excavates a site, he is not
so much interested in finding museum specimens as he
is in solving the riddles of the past. This involves a
careful, inch-by-inch survey of each level of the site.
The order in which objects lie in a mound is of crucial
importance for dating and interpretation. But a pot-
hunter simply digs in gaily, ignoring anything that does
not promise a cash return—though such things are of
vital value to archaeologists.

Today, most of the important mounds are protected
by law from such vandalism. Unhappily those laws are
quite recent, and for more than a century some of the
major mounds were plundered again and again. A
classical archaeological horror story is the fate of the
Spiro Mound in Oklahoma, a large temple mound at the

extreme western margin of the Temple Mound region.

It was a farmer of the last century who discovered that the Spiro Mound held treasure of the past. Plowing at the base of the hill, he struck something hard in the ground and stopped to examine it. It was a reddish piece of stone, pipe-shaped, with tobacco ashes in its bowl.

He showed it to some of his friends, and later that year, after the harvest was out of the way, they went back to dig in the mound. "Indian relics" were in good demand in the East, where collectors paid well for them. So the farmer and his friends began by chopping down all the trees on the mound, thus making it impossible ever to date the mound exactly. (Archaeologists, by counting tree rings or by estimating the age of the trees that had grown on the mound since it was sealed, could have made good use of those trees.)

The diggers were rewarded wherever they thrust in a spade. More sculptured stone pipes, dark pottery, sheets of copper, beads of stone and shell and bone, axes, and maces—the mound was a storehouse of treasure. Unhappily, some of the objects disintegrated as soon as they were exposed to the air, since the pothunters had no idea of how to preserve them. But no matter; there were plenty more, so such losses failed to discourage them.

Word soon got around that the Spiro Mound was being mined for archaeological artifacts. The University of Oklahoma, which naturally is a center of archaeological activity in that state, sent men out to the mound to investigate. But the university people found that the pothunters had formed a mining company and incorporated. The mound was their property, and they intended to work it for all it was worth.

To the horror of all professional archaeologists, the treasure hunters proceeded to dynamite the mound open, the more easily to get at the salable artifacts it contained. The Spiro Mound was almost irreparably spoiled as an archaeological site through the carelessness of the men who exploited it. Later, the State Legislature decreed that private digging in ancient sites was not in the public interest, and today anyone in Oklahoma who finds such a site must report it to the University of Oklahoma's Department of Anthropology, which will license only qualified excavators. Since 1935, the University has carried on excavations of its own at Spiro. This work has been of great value—though most of the mound was ruined before the archaeologists could get to it.

All through the states where mound builders once lived, amateur archaeologists—"Sunday diggers"—have done their bit to harass university people. Still, many of the mounds have yielded information of benefit and worth. Today, teams of archaeologists are at work every year in the mound country, laboriously sifting through the mountains of earth, striving to unravel some of the many riddles of these long-vanished builders of mounds and temples.

7

SUNS AND STINKARDS

THE END OF THE TEMPLE MOUND CULTURE IS MYSTE-rious, and perhaps we will never know why it came so suddenly. In some places, though, the old ways lingered on among the Indians of the Southeast.

Here, in this warm, fertile country, certain Indian tribes continued to carry on their rituals and folkways long after the coming of the white man. This was canebrake country, where jointed stalks of cane, thirty feet high in some places, sprouted thickly for hundreds of miles. Food was abundant here, and the Indians had the leisure to develop elaborate customs and po-litical units.

When the white man came to the Southeast, he found a loose confederation of tribes in Georgia and Alabama, amounting to some thirty thousand Indians in fifty good-sized towns. The dominant Indians of this con-federation called themselves the Muskhogee, but English traders, meeting a branch of the Muskhogee who lived along the Ocheese Creek, called them Creek Indians, and as Creeks they have since been known.

Other Indian tribes in the same general part of the continent spoke related Muskhogean languages, though they were not necessarily related to the Creeks in any other way. There were the Chickasaw, wide-ranging and fond of quarreling; the Choctaw, farmers who liked to stay on their own land; the Cherokee, largest of all the tribes, with a population of over twenty thousand, and many others. The Cherokee spoke a language similar to that of the Iroquois, which leads us to think that perhaps the Iroquois came out of the South sometime in the far past.

All these Muskhogean tribes lived in what, a few centuries before, had been Temple Mound country. The Creek and the Cherokee, particularly, liked to live in the vicinity of the old mounds. They had no traditions dealing with the mounds, except the vague impression that they were very ancient. They built mounds of their own sometimes, small ones, on which the chief's home was usually placed.

One particular Muskhogean tribe living along the Mississippi is of special interest to us because of its social structure, which quite probably was a direct survival of the Temple Mound culture. This tribe was the Natchez, about whom we know a great deal, thanks to Frenchmen who lived with them and studied them from 1698 to 1732. The Natchez were not a particularly large tribe—there were only four thousand of them—but they are interesting as the last representatives of the Temple Mound people.

The Natchez lived in seven small villages grouped

Tattooed Natchez Indian

around Emerald Mound, an imposing, thirty-five-foot-high mound covering seven acres, and obviously patterned after a Mexican model. Natchez social life, too, seemed to owe a great deal to the ideas of the Aztec and Maya, but it had a few features that were unique and thoroughly fascinating.

The Natchez government was an absolute monarchy. At its head was a ruler called the Great Sun, who was considered divine, a descendant of the Sun itself. The Great Sun had total power over his subjects. According to a French observer of two hundred fifty years ago: "When he [the Great Sun] gives the leavings of his dinner to his brothers or any of his relatives, he pushes the dishes to them with his feet. . . . The submissiveness of the savages to their chief, who commands them with the most despotic power, is extreme . . . if he demands the life of any one of them he [the victim] comes himself to present his head."

Clad in his regal crown of swan feathers, the Great Sun was carried everywhere on a litter. His foot never touched the bare earth. When he had to walk, mats were spread before him. He and a few priests were the only ones permitted to enter the temple atop the mound, where an eternal fire burned and the bones of previous Great Suns were kept. When a Great Sun died, his entire household—wife and slaves—was killed to accompany him in the afterlife.

The immediate relatives of the Great Sun—his brothers, sisters, uncles, and so on—were members of a privileged class called "Suns." All of the important functionaries of the tribe were chosen from the ranks of the Suns, who were regarded with the greatest deference by the lower orders.

Beneath the Suns in importance was a class called the "Nobles." Beneath them were the Honored Men, and below them was a large body of despised and downtrodden commoners known by the uncomplimentary name of "Stinkards." The class divisions were sharply drawn and it was impossible for a Natchez to move from the class he was born in to another.

The unusual feature of this class system is the way it revolved from generation to generation. All Suns, including the Great Sun himself, were required to choose their mates from the Stinkard class! Every Sun was thus the offspring of a Sun and a Stinkard. The children of woman Suns married to Stinkards were Suns themselves, but the children of male Suns were demoted to the Noble class.

Thus the son of the Great Sun could never succeed his father, since he would be only a Noble. The Great Sun's successor was usually the son of one of his sisters, since Sun rank descended only through the female line.

The children of Nobles also had to marry Stinkards. Again, the offspring of female Nobles were Nobles also, but the children of male Nobles were demoted another class, to Honored Men. It worked the same way among them: the children of male Honored Men became Stinkards.

Since there were always a great many more Stinkards than members of the three upper classes, most Stinkards married other Stinkards, and their children, of course, were Stinkards, too. But a good many Stinkards were selected as mates for Suns, Nobles, and Honored Men, and so their children rose in class.

The ones whose lot was least enviable were the Stinkard men who married Sun women. Although their children were Suns, these men had no power themselves, and were regarded simply as breeding creatures. They could not eat with their Sun wives, had to stand in their presence like servants, and might at any time be executed on a whim and replaced by another Stinkard.

As with the Iroquois and so many other Indians, the men ruled, but the power of descent was through the female line. Female Suns chose the new Great Sun; females alone could give their rank to their children.

It was an intricate and clever system which guaranteed a constant transfusion of new blood into each of the four classes, preventing any of the abuses that develop when such a class system becomes frozen forever.

Whether this unusual arrangement was common to all the Temple Mound peoples will never be known. But it seems safe to say that some sort of class system was found among them all, and probably an absolute monarchy as well. It could be that only the Natchez, the last survivors, went on to evolve their original and exceptional system of descent.

For a long time the relations between the Natchez and the French settlers of Mississippi were cordial. In 1729, however, the Natchez launched a massacre against the French which ended, as such things usually did, with the complete destruction of the Natchez civilization. The tribe was nearly exterminated, and the few survivors were dispersed to take up lodging with other Indians of the Southeast, among whom they had reputations for mystical powers.

These other tribes—the Choctaw, Chickasaw, Creek, and Cherokee—had much better relations with the white men, and remained relatively intact for a century after the destruction of the Natchez. Unlike the Natchez, these tribes were probably late-comers to the area, not arriving until the final days of the Temple Mound Culture. Yet all of them took over certain features of the older way of life.

Wherever life is easy, complex patterns of culture can develop. In the fertile Southeast, with its abun-

dance of nuts, berries, roots, birds, and fish, there was no trouble obtaining food. The Creeks and their neighbors did some farming, but they had plenty of time for games and religious observance.

A typical Creek town was arranged around an open plaza, with the chief's house at one end and a ceremonial building at the other. These important houses were usually elevated on low mounds. The streets were often straight and well laid out. Each house had its own garden plot where vegetables were raised, but the main fields, divided into family plots, were outside the town.

The center of the plaza contained two important features: the Hot House, or winter temple, and the open court where the game of *chungke* was played.

The Hot House was a round building fifty feet in diameter, plastered with mud. A fire burned constantly inside, but there was no smoke hole, and the atmosphere could hardly have been pleasant. Women never entered the Hot House. In it, each warrior of the tribe had his own bench, and there he would go to smoke his pipe or rest or talk with his friends—a kind of men's club. An adjoining open cabin served the same purpose in the summer, when heat made the Hot House unbearable. The Creek warriors wore few clothes, but decorated themselves with tattoos that often covered almost their entire bodies. They would shave their heads in curious patterns, leaving the head bald on one side, or in front, or providing a top scalp lock as a challenge to enemies.

Chungke, or "chunkey," was the popular game of the Southeast, and it seems to be of great antiquity, going back to Hopewell and Adena times. It was played by two men who used eight-foot poles tapered to flat points at their ends. One man would bowl a stone disk, an inch and a half thick and five inches across, down the field, and both players, running abreast, would hurl their poles javelin-fashion toward the stone. The player whose stick landed closer to the point where the

stone stopped rolling scored a point; if his pole actually touched the stone, he tallied two points. The Creek would play chungke endlessly, betting high stakes on the outcome of each match.

Another popular Southeastern game—one which the white man has borrowed—was lacrosse. Balls of leather were used, and the players, about sixty on a team, used sticks with small thong-laced scoops at one end. It was forbidden to touch the ball with the hands. The idea was to scoop the ball up, carry it, and throw it through goalposts at the ends of the five-hundred-yard-long field. Twenty goals was game. There were hardly any rules other than these. Bodily contact was lively; broken arms and legs, frequent.

The Southeastern Indians had a clan system much like that of the Iroquois, except that instead of eight clans there were about fifty. They were divided into two groups, the "Whites" and the "Reds," but these were not moieties in the Iroquois fashion, since one did not have to marry into the opposite moiety. Marriage within one's own clan, however, was prohibited.

The division into White Clans and Red Clans was paralleled by other such twofold groupings. Among the Creek, there were Upper Towns and Lower Towns, the Upper also being known as the Peace Towns, the Lower as the War Towns. The White Clans were Peace Clans; the Red, War Clans.

In theory, all the peacetime responsibilities of Creek life were assigned to the White Clans of the Upper Towns. The Miko, or principal chief of the confederacy, was always chosen from a White Clan. White Towns were sanctuaries for fleeing murderers. The clansmen of the Upper Towns were charged with carrying out such civil ceremonies as the *puskita,* the eight-day summer corn-harvest festival. On the other hand, all the ceremonies of war were the affair of the Lower Towns; members of the Red Clans were supposed to organize war parties, lead raiding expeditions, and take care of the religious rituals having to do with war, which in the Southeast was something combining aspects of play and religion rather than a matter of conquest or extermination.

This division between Upper Towns and Lower

Towns soon became blurred geographically, and many of the Lower Towns were actually north of the Upper Towns as some tribes changed residences. And in most villages both Red and White Clans could be found. The chief, though, always came from a White Clan.

The Creek had a caste system, but it was by no means as complicated as that of the Natchez. There was no hereditary nobility. The highest caste, called the Beloved Men, consisted of those who had distinguished themselves by their wisdom or their valor, and the rank was not passed on from generation to generation.

Descent in the Creek and other Southeast tribes was once again through the mother. This seems to be true in many agricultural societies, where the women, who do the bulk of the work in the fields, take official ownership of the lands and houses of the tribe, though the men still retain their responsibilities of decision-making and warfare.

The head of each Creek household was the brother of the head woman. Naturally, he lived with the family of his own wife, not with his sister's family, but he was required to return to his sister's house to undertake the education of his nephews. His sister's husband, meanwhile, was bringing up *his* nephews. Strange to us, perhaps, but not to those born into such a way of life.

Creek education was unusually strict. Boys had to bathe every morning in the creek nearest the village, no matter how icy the water. In winter they broke the ice in order to bathe. When a child misbehaved, his arms and legs would be scratched with implements made from the teeth of garfish. Sometimes boys would be scratched even when they had done nothing wrong, simply to toughen them up. Serious offenses were punished by severe whipping.

Marriages were always arranged by the women. Neither the fathers nor the young people themselves were consulted. The marriage ceremony consisted of the bridegroom's handing his bride a deer's foot and half an ear of corn. But the marriage was not official until the young husband had slain a deer and brought it home, and the bride had carried it into their house, cooked it, and fed her husband the meat before witnesses.

When a man married, he went to live with his wife's family. As in some other tribes, the Creek had a particularly strong mother-in-law taboo, and a man was supposed to avoid his wife's mother as much as possible. If a man's wife died, his wife's clan tried to find him a new wife after the one-year mourning period had elapsed. If no one were available, the clan officially "set him free" in a special ceremony and he could choose a wife elsewhere. When a man died, his wife was forbidden to remarry for *four* years, unless she agreed to marry her late husband's brother. The brother was required to take her if she requested it, even if he had a wife of his own. (This could sometimes result in a man's being married to women of two different clans, and he would have to divide his time between their separate lodgings.)

Death, which had been so major a part of mound-builder life, continued to hold great importance for the Muskhogean Indians who took over the mound builders' territories. The Creek had lengthy funeral ceremonies in which the body was buried accompanied by expensive offerings, and the house of the dead person was purified through rituals and the wails of hired mourners. The Choctaw and Natchez would leave bodies exposed on platforms until vultures had picked away all the flesh, and then, hearkening back to customs two thousand years old in that region, would bury them in mounds of earth.

These Southeastern Indians had much in common with the Iroquois, both in their elaborate political organizations and in their fondness for war and torture. As with the Iroquois, the Creek and others were commando raiders who swooped down, brandishing spiked clubs, in lightning raids. "They never face their enemies in open field, which they say is great folly in the English," one observer noted, "but sulk from one covert to another." They also practiced the unattractive custom of bringing captives back to the village, staking them out in the main square, and torturing them to death while the whole populace watched eagerly.

The Southeast Indians were similar to the Iroquois in their attitude toward the spirit world. They, too, saw themselves as surrounded by hundreds of spirits: spirits of earth and air, of plants and animals. Beyond them all was the Master of Breath, who had created man. Not only he, but all the other spirits, had to be placated with offerings and ceremonies.

The Creek believed that certain animal spirits brought specific diseases to man. Headache, for example, was caused by mice, and the Creek shaman would chant a formula addressed to the mouse spirits:

> *Gallop away, gallop away, gallop away!*
> *Red rat, red cloud.*
> *My head is hot, is roaring!*

The neighboring Cherokee carried the idea a step further. Animal spirits, in revenge for being slaughtered by humans, sent disease, but plant spirits provided remedies. Cherokee shamans would chew special plant roots, such as that of the ginseng, and spurt the root onto the sufferer while chanting the magic formulas of relief.

Those shamans who were most successful at curing the sick gained widespread reputations. They would travel from village to village, performing their services. During the round of festivals that marked the Indian year, these important shamans took charge of the rituals.

Every year at the time of the first corn harvest the Creek would hold their most important festival, the *puskita* or "busk." Homes were swept, old fires extinguished, new ones lit. In the plaza, men purged themselves by taking the "black drink," an herb tea made of the leaves of a shrub called *Ilex cassine,* which induced vomiting. For four days they would fast, until their bodies had been completely cleansed.

At the festival time, all crimes were forgiven except that of murder. New laws were adopted. Boys entering manhood were given new names, and were scratched with fish teeth to prove their maturity. Dancing and games went on far into the night. One common Creek dance was the Snake Dance, which the whites called the "stomp dance." Men and women formed a circle around a fire, hands on each other's shoulders, bellowing out responses to a song chanted by a leader. Some of the Creek who have kept the old ways into the twentieth century still perform the Snake Dance and a few of the other ancient rites.

They perform them, though, in Oklahoma, far from their ancestral territories. For the Creek, the Choctaw, the Chickasaw, and the Cherokee were dispossessed from their lands more than a hundred and thirty years ago.

It was too much to expect that the white man would have left the Indians of the Southeast on their native soil. The prize was too tempting. Consider this report on the Creek lands, filed in 1791 by a scout of the brand-new United States Government:

The territory, he said, was "remarkably healthy. . . . The constant breezes, which are probably occasioned by the high hills and numerous rapid water-courses, render the heat of summer very temperate; and towards autumn they are delightfully perfumed by the ripening aromatic shrubbery, which abounds throughout the country. . . . The winters are soft and mild, and the summers sweet and wholesome. . . . The country possesses every species of wood and clay proper for building, and the soil and climate seem well suited to the culture of corn, wine, oil, silk, hemp, rice, wheat, tobacco, indigo, every species of fruit trees. . . ."

Unfortunately, he reported, the area was currently "rendered unpleasant by being in possession of the jealous natives." But he had no doubt that it "must, in process of time, become a most delectable part of the United States."

The Choctaw, Chickasaw, Creek, and Cherokee had weathered the coming of the white man fairly well. Unlike the Natchez, who had tried to fight, and who had been destroyed, the other tribes formed alliances with the invaders, who rewarded them with the collective title of the Four Civilized Tribes. (They became Five Civilized Tribes in the eighteenth century, when a group of rebellious Creek split away and retired to the Florida swamps, receiving the name of Seminole, "Those Who Ran Away.")

The Choctaw allied themselves to the French. The Chickasaw and Cherokee became friends of the English. The Creek, largest and most powerful of the confederacies, leaned now toward the English who had come into Georgia, now toward the Spaniards in Florida. All of them learned things from the white man, and flourished and expanded through the middle of the eighteenth century. But during the Revolutionary War, most of these Southeastern Indians backed their English allies against the rebellious colonists. It was a fatal error in judgment.

The British were defeated, and left. Now the Indians were in the hands of the settlers, who came flooding into their lands, pushing them ruthlessly aside. By 1803, Opothle, the Miko of the Creek, lamented, "What land we have left is but large enough to live and walk on."

But the worst was ahead. The process of dispossessing the Indians, which had been unofficial and irregular, became legal in 1830 when Congress passed a law confiscating all Indian land east of the Mississippi, and authorizing the removal of the Indians, at government expense, to land in the West.

A tragic emigration began for the Five Civilized Tribes, not without bloodshed and anguish. Thousands of Seminole in the impenetrable Florida Everglades fought off United States soldiers for five years, and finally won out; they are still there. The Cherokee, who also refused to move, were expelled by soldiers, even though they petitioned Congress, saying, "Are we to be hunted through the mountains like wild beasts?"

The unhappy Indians ultimately had to yield. By 1840, the remnants of the Five Civilized Tribes had relocated themselves in what is now Oklahoma, after a journey still known as The Trail of Tears. Thousands had died en route to the wilderness where they were

condemned to live. As they sadly left the land that had
been theirs for centuries, they sang this mournful song:

> I have no more land.
> I am driven away from home
> Driven up the red waters
> Let us all go.
> Let us all die together. . . .

But they did not all die together. They built a new
life for themselves in western Oklahoma, despite further inroads of the white man too complicated and too
saddening to chronicle here. Today, the Five Civilized
Tribes hold considerable power in Oklahoma, and
many of them are educated and prosperous. They have
not, though, forgotten the old days when their fathers
lived in Georgia and Alabama and Mississippi. They
come together still for festivals, arriving by car, train,
and plane, and dance and sing and tell tales of the
time when a man could smoke his pipe in peace at the
Hot House, when the old festivals still had meaning,
when authority descended not from the White House in
Washington but from the Miko's house atop the mound
at one end of the quiet village plaza.

8

SMOKERS OF
THE PEACE PIPE

IN THE GREAT UPPER MIDLANDS OF NORTH AMERICA, the area that now is Wisconsin and Michigan and upper Illinois, Minnesota, Kansas, Nebraska, and on westward to where the plains begin, a host of Indian tribes dwelt in the days before the white man came. Each of those tribes had its own dialect, its own customs and folkways. Each one considered itself quite different from all the other tribes of the region.

Yet we, looking down on these Middle Western tribes from the viewpoint of history, tend to blur them into a single group. They all look alike to us. Since they built no spectacular mounds, organized no elaborate confederations, left no remarkable museum pieces, we dismiss them as "just farmers."

And so they were, just farmers. But if we examined each tribe in detail, we would see that each had its own history, its own heroes, its own individuality. Each was jealously proud of its identity. Unfair as it is, we have

120

to let them merge into one large vague group, "just farmers," and we cannot linger long with them.

They came into their territory early. In 1931, workers building a road in Minnesota came upon the skeleton of a teen-aged girl buried in clay laid down by a glacial lake some eleven thousand years ago. We know, too, of those mysteriously precocious copper-working people who lived between Lake Michigan and Lake Superior at a time when Egypt's pyramids were yet unbuilt. There were agricultural peoples in the Great Lakes region in the time of Christ.

To the south lived the Adena-Hopewell Culture, and there certainly must have been contact between the mound builders and the Indians of the colder country by the year A.D. 350. Very likely the languages spoken in that part of the world then were of the Siouan family, but the Siouans did not remain around the Great Lakes. They moved westward into the Plains region, where we shall meet them in the next chapter.

The dispossessors of the Siouans were Indians who spoke an Algonquian language. They probably came from the eastern seaboard more than a thousand years ago. It is important to understand that we are dealing with spans of many centuries, and woodland peoples simply do not stay put for thousands of years. As they exhaust their hunting territories, they pull up stakes and head for new lands.

So we must try to visualize a constant ebb and flow of peoples. As we have seen, all of the Indians came out of Asia originally and spread out over the two American continents. One group, whom we call the Algonquians, made it all the way to the Atlantic Coast. But then some of them began to migrate *westward* again, pushing the Siouan people of the Great Lakes area westward also. At one time the whole northern part of North America east of the Mississippi must have comprised one great Algonquian zone. Then (we can guess it happened about seven hundred years ago, but it may have been earlier) the Iroquoians came up out of the Southwest to drive a wedge between the Algonquians of the coast and those of the Middle West.

Those Algonquians of the Middle West have tribal traditions that tell of having come from the East, many years ago, to oust other Indians. These misty traditions are the closest we can come to Indian history.

The anthropologist Ruth Underhill has given these western Algonquians and their neighbors the general title of "People of the Calumet"—People of the Peace Pipe. It is a good name, for it serves to provide a common tag for tribes of different customs and languages.

All these Indians smoked a stone pipe with a feathered stem, which the French called *chalumeau,* the Indians *calumet.* Carved from soft red stone, decorated with loving care, the calumet had a sacred meaning to these Indians. "The sceptres of our kings are not so much respected," the explorer Marquette wrote. The pipe was smoked on many occasions—to ratify treaties, to welcome strangers, to signify the declaration of war or peace. An Indian about to set out on a risky journey would smoke the calumet first, to win the favor of the gods, and particularly *the* god, Manitou, the Great Spirit, whom all these Indian nations worshiped. And so Longfellow tells us in *Hiawatha:*

> On the Mountains of the Prairie
> Gitche Manitou the mighty . . .
> Stood erect and called the nations
> Called the tribes of men together. . . .
>
> And, erect upon the mountains
> Gitche Manitou the mighty
> Smoked the calumet, the Peace-Pipe.

Longfellow's Hiawatha, though he bore the name of a famous Iroquois, was actually a fictionalized member of the Algonquian tribe known as the Ojibwa. The Ojibwa were the largest and most powerful of the Midwestern tribes, but they suffered a peculiar humiliation at the hands of the white men. The European invaders, unable to pronounce the name of the tribe, garbled it into "Chippeway," and stuck to their mispronunciation so stubbornly that the Ojibwa finally gave up in despair and started using it themselves! Many Ojibwa today call themselves Chippeway.

They came in from the north and east and took over the territory around Lakes Huron and Superior, extending through Minnesota and Dakota and into Canada. The land was occupied when the Ojibwa arrived; the Siouan-speaking Winnebago were there, the Sauk and Foxes, the Kickapoo and the Menominee. The Ojibwa forced these other tribes westward and took over their farmland. It was a cold, harsh country, but it could be

made to yield food. The broad, deep lakes surrendered
a generous harvest of fish, and the forests thronged with
elk and deer. In the shallow small lakes that were so
numerous, wild rice grew in easily gathered abundance.
Like their cousin Algonquians in the eastern woodlands, the Ojibwa lived primarily by hunting and fishing; farming, the women's work, filled in the gaps in
the diet.

To the south farming was more important. The Miami
Confederacy of Indiana and Illinois, Algonquians also,
cultivated corn, beans, and squash, and in the fertile
river-bottom land the crops were wonderfully copious.
One Miami village along the Wabash had five or six
miles of farmland under its care. (There was another
village of the Miamis whose Indian name, meaning
"Skunk Place," is still in use. It is Chicago.) While the
women of the Miamis tended the fields, the men hunted
and fished, and several weeks each year moved out into
the prairie lands to hunt buffalo. They had to make
these expeditions on foot, since the horse had become
extinct in North America thousands of years before,
and would not be known there again until the white
men reintroduced it. Each fall, the Miamis would enter
the prairies and set fire to the dry grass, panicking the
herds, who could be cut off and slain with bow and arrow. The kill ran as high as two hundred buffalo a day.

The various Algonquians of the Middle West were
not very different from the Eastern Algonquians in
matters of clothing, housing, or equipment. But they
had no birch bark except north of Michigan and so

could not build either the light, graceful canoes of the East, or the easily dismantled tipis and wigwams. They covered their houses with mats or rough elm bark, and built their canoes from heavy butternut wood.

The Algonquians of the Middle West were subject to influences from all sides. On the far side of the Mississippi were tribes who spoke Siouan languages—the Osage, Iowa, and Missouri. The Ojibwa and their cousins traded and sometimes fought with these Westerners. To the south along the Mississippi had once been the Temple Mound people, and more recently the Choctaw and Chickasaw. On the east were the Iroquois and such Iroquoian tribes as the Erie, the Shawnee, and the Huron. The Ojibwa were frequently at war with the Iroquoians and finally drove them out of the Great Lakes area. Even the fierce Five Nations of the Iroquois themselves met their match when they attempted to extend their sway into Ojibwa territory.

With all these different tribes surrounding them, the Algonquians of the Middle West borrowed from all sides. Their most notable adoption was that of the stone pipe, a Hopewell specialty. The Hopewells had for hundreds of years obtained their pipestone from a quarry in Minnesota. The Algonquians, moving into Minnesota long after the Hopewell Culture had vanished, continued to use the soft red stone for pipes, and gradually learned how to fit it to a long reed to make the famous calumet.

The Western Algonquians also had a clan system, something the Easterners did not bother with. Clan descent, though, was patrilineal instead of matrilineal, meaning that a child became a member of his father's clan, not his mother's as with the Iroquois. Most of the Algonquians also divided their clans into moieties, but they never seemed to grasp the real purpose of such a division, which is to segregate family groups and prevent a person from marrying a close relative. An Algonquian family would assign its children alternately to one moiety and then the other, so no family segregation ever developed. But it was necessary, at least, to marry outside one's own clan.

Most of the Middle Western tribes had a chief who held considerable power, though he was never the kind of absolute monarch found among the Natchez. Some of the Algonquian tribes borrowed the system of the Siouan Winnebago, who had two leaders of equal power, the war chief and the peace chief.

Calumets were of two sorts also: war pipes and peace pipes. The peace calumet not only served to formalize treaties, but was a kind of passport. "Carry it about with you and show it," one European priest wrote, "and you can march fearlessly amid enemies who, even in the heat of battle, lay down their arms when it was shown." The red-feathered calumet of war had the opposite effect; it was taken down and smoked only when tempers were high, and after it had passed from hand to hand, the warriors of the tribe would be eager for action.

All of the Indians of the Middle West fought, even the generally mild and peaceful Miami. We, who think of war as a matter of tanks and bombs, regard it only as a last resort when all other means of disputes fail, but among most Indian tribes it was a ritualistic event, a way of proving manhood, and had little or nothing to do with boundary disputes or the desire for conquest. (At least, not until the white man came. War then became a matter of desperate self-defense against a powerful invader. And some of the Indians, like the Iroquois and the Creek, learned white man's ways and began to war on their neighbors for the sake of subjugating them.)

When the time came to smoke the war calumet, the warriors went forth in small bands for a commando raid, after a feast and a prayer meeting. The leader of the war party carried with him a sacred bundle, containing animal skins and bones, certain plants, and other objects considered holy.

As in the East, a good deal of scalping took place. But the most valorous feat of all was to touch a live enemy in the midst of his comrades. When the warriors returned home, they would rise at village feasts to boast of their prowess. In dance and song, they would re-enact the hunting of the enemy, the attack, the moment of conflict. A brave might sing:

> This is how I clubbed him down
> He fell and cried out for mercy
> But I would not spare him, I showed no pity
> For he was my enemy.

Like the Iroquois, these Midwestern Indians often took prisoners. But most of them took women and children rather than men, since few warriors would allow themselves to be captured, and usually fought to the death. Such captives as were taken were made slaves, instead of being tortured to death.

The belief in the Manitou, or Great Spirit, was universal in the area. Some tribes called him the Giver of Breath, others the Master of Life, but the general concept was the same: that of a kind and benevolent creator-spirit. There were other deities too, such as Manabush, the Great Rabbit, a comic, clowning creature whose exploits in righting wrongs often had a wildly bizarre flavor.

A boy's first encounter with the supernatural world came when he was eleven or twelve, and he was sent forth to have a vision. Blackening his face with a charred stick, he would venture alone into the woods and remain there, fasting and praying, until some powerful spirit came and spoke to him. Sometimes days would pass before the boy, weakened and dizzy from his lonely vigil, received the longed-for vision and could return.

Originally religious matters among these tribes were in the hands of one or two men in each village, shamans who had established a reputation for regularly receiving spirit visions. These men performed the necessary rituals, uttered the required prayers, and visited the sick.

Later, an elaborate society of medicine men sprang up, called the "Midewiwin," or Grand Medicine Society. It began among the Ojibwa and Winnebago, but rapidly spread to the other tribes. The organization was very complicated, with many different ranks, and a vast lore written in strange symbols on strips of birch bark. Many experts feel that the Midewiwin, though its roots may go back five hundred years or more, did not really start to develop until Jesuit priests entered the Great Lakes region. The Indians then adapted some of the organizational ideas of the Roman Catholic Church to their own rites and beliefs, and the result was the intricate structure of the Grand Medicine Society.

The white men did not disrupt the peace-pipe peoples as they did the Indians of New England or the Southeast. For almost two centuries after the newcomers arrived, the Ojibwa and Winnebago and Kickapoo and their neighbors managed to hold their own, trading with the white men, occasionally fighting with them, but remaining on their own land. Their ways changed, as they learned how to use the white man's steel tools and his guns (and his liquor). The French, who were the chief occupants of the region at first, were more interested in trade than in colonization, and so did not attempt to drive the red men out. Many French traders married Indian wives.

In 1763, the French lost their American possessions and left the country. The Indians of the Middle West, who now wore white man's clothes and suffered from white man's diseases, tried to seize the opportunity to return to their old way of life. Pontiac, a chief of the Ottawa (an Algonquian tribe closely related to the Ojibwa) organized a joint effort to drive the English from their territory. An alliance of Ottawa, Ojibwa, Shawnee, Delaware, and some Iroquoian tribes was briefly successful, but by 1769 Pontiac was dead and the alliance disrupted.

When the American Revolution came, the Indians, choosing what they felt was the lesser of two evils, supported the British against the buckskin-wearing settlers. Thirty years of warfare followed, and some tribes, such as the Shawnee, the Delaware, and the Miami, faded away almost entirely. After 1812, much of the Indian land was bought by the American Government, and some was simply taken away. Today, there are thousands of Ojibwa still living on reservations in Minnesota and Wisconsin, and there are some Winnebago in Nebraska, Ottawa in Oklahoma, and Kickapoo in Kansas. Here and there in Iowa, Michigan, and Montana there are scattered pockets of displaced Algonquians. Most of the survivors of the small tribes have ended their wanderings in Oklahoma. Smallpox epidemics in the nineteenth century greatly reduced their numbers.

There was nothing particularly unusual or distinguished about the Ojibwa, the Winnebago, the Kickapoo, and the rest of these Indians who once held sway in the Middle West. They farmed, they hunted, they made war on each other, they smoked their pipes of peace and war—and ultimately most of them lost out to the white men who now live on the lands that for eight or ten thousand years had been Indian property. Though they had no great artistic or architectural achievements to match the accomplishments of some other Indians, they had a way of life, a code, a religion. They were important and interesting to themselves, if not to outsiders. Today, Christianized and "civilized," they live like white men, and the woods no longer resound to war songs like this one of the Winnebago:

> Sun and earth are everlasting
> Men must die!
> Old age is a thing of evil
> Charge and die!

9

INDIANS OF
THE PLAINS

WHAT IMAGE COMES TO YOUR MIND WHEN YOU HEAR
the word "Indian"?

The chances are extremely good that you immediately picture an Indian of the Great Plains, mounted bareback on a fast-moving mustang, clad in leggings and beaded vest and massive feather headdress, galloping across the plains, spear in hand, toward an enormous herd of buffalo. It is an image firmly planted by Hollywood. It is accurate enough as far as it goes: all through the nineteenth century, the pioneers of the Great Plains encountered Indians looking just that way. But in the long view of history those spear-wielding, horseback-riding Plains Indians held the center of the stage only for a moment. In a way, they were creations of the white man, who gave them horses, who taught them how to make spears of iron, who even sold them the beads with which they decorated their leggings. Life on the Great Plains was quite a different thing before the white man arrived to change it.

132

The first white man to enter the Great Plains was Coronado. He started northward from Mexico City in 1540, in search of the Seven Cities of Cibola, which were supposed to be brimming with riches of every kind. (*"Cibola"* is the Spanish word for buffalo.) He entered the Pueblo country of what is now New Mexico, and was told constantly that the golden cities were "further on." So onward he went, deep into the heart of the North American continent, but there were no cities of gold in those vast grasslands, and finally he turned back disappointed.

Coronado reported that he had found two sorts of Indians in the sprawling prairie lands. One kind, he said, "travel the plains with the cows [buffalo]," living in tents "like Arabs." These were nomads. "They neither sow nor reap corn," Coronado said of them. Probably they were the Apache, who belong in a later chapter.

The other kind of Indian lived in permanent villages made up of round, straw-thatched houses, grouped in river valleys. They were farmers, cultivating corn and beans, and such hunting as they did was only a part-time occupation. Though it may come as a surprise to those whose idea of Indian history has been formed by the movies, these settled farmers of Coronado's were the Sioux—the Sioux who, three centuries later, would become the mounted, buffalo-hunting terrors of the West. The first way of life in the Great Plains was agricultural.

The Great Plains are actually three separate regions

which form a sweeping flatland of staggering size between the Mississippi and the Rocky Mountains. To the
east is rolling prairie land, today the corn country of
Kansas and Nebraska. Then rise the high plains of the
Dakotas, eastern Wyoming and Colorado; and finally,
the barren, rugged foothills of the Rockies. Much of this
central region is dry and dusty, though not so dry as it
once was.

Nor is it as moist, either. Ten thousand years ago, both
the Southwest and the western Plains were lands of
lakes and forests and heavy rain. Folsom Man roamed
then, leaving a trail of points behind him. As the land
dried out and the open country turned to a great dust
bowl, the hunters retreated, and perhaps for several
thousand years no one lived in the Great Plains at all.
Important cultures were developing on the border of
the Plains—in the Southwest, the Pueblo people; to the
southeast, the mound builders—but the center of the
continent was uninhabited save for a few tribes of
nomads.

About a thousand years ago, certain Indian tribes
began to nibble gingerly at the edges of this vast empty
domain. By that time, agriculture was well advanced,
and the Indians had bred varieties of corn which could
survive in the relatively dry and cold northern reaches
of the Plains. A slow migration into the Plains began, a
westward move out of Hopewell territory all along the
Mississippi, and from the Southwest eastward. Between A.D. 1200 and A.D. 1600, thousands of Indians
took possession of the Plains, converging from all sides,

south and east and west, and to some extent from the north.

The Indians who moved into the Plains did some hunting, since the Plains were occupied by incredibly large herds of buffalo, but farming was their main business. The later Indian inhabitants of the Plains called these first-comers the Village Tribes or the Old Settlers.

The Old Settlers who came in from the South and East spoke languages different from the Algonquian tongues of the Great Lakes or the Muskhogean tongues of the Southwest. Their languages fall into two categories: Siouan and Caddoan. Both these language families have some relation to Iroquoian, and a more distant link to Muskhogean, which indicates that the Old Settlers came out of the southern part of the continent.

It ought to be made clear that there was never any one tribe called the Sioux. The word is a French term meaning "a tribe of enemies," and was originally applied to many tribes of Plains Indians, particularly those of the Dakota Confederation. The tribes specifically referred to as Sioux included the Tetons, Brulès, Hunkpapas, Yanktons, Santees, Sissetons, and half a dozen others. Gradually the term "Sioux" began to be applied to all those Indians of the Plains whose language fitted into the family known as "Siouan," and so many of the traditional enemies of the Dakota Confederation came to be called "Sioux" simply for reasons of language grouping. Today, most Indians of the Siouan tribes are content to identify themselves to outsiders as "Sioux," rather than try to explain the basic inaccuracy involved.

The Siouan Indians came into the prairies out of the Mississippi and Ohio valleys, bringing with them the traditions of agriculture practiced by the mound builders. The closely related Caddoan peoples came from the same general area, and spread far to the north, dividing into subtribes and taking possession of fertile river land in the Dakotas. Here we find such tribes as the Arikara, the Pawnee, the Wichita.

The Old Settlers raised tobacco, beans, corn, and squash. When they could spare the time, they went on hunting forays to bring back buffalo meat. But it was no easy matter to hunt these bulky beasts on foot. A stampeding herd of eighteen-hundred-pound buffalo presented great challenges to the huntsmen, whose bows and arrows often proved too puny for the job. One frequently successful method was to panic a herd and drive it over a cliff, a technique whose venerable ancestry went back at least ten thousand years to Folsom days. The Old Settlers made only one or two hunting trips a year, staying close to their villages most of the time.

Those villages consisted of sod huts. There was no elm or birch bark on the nearly treeless Plains, so the Old Settlers built their houses of a framework of small logs covered over with brush and then with a thick, hard-packed layer of earth. The sturdy huts stood up well against the fierce winter weather, and many a white settler built his home in the Indian manner.

There are still some Plains people today—whites—who live in sod houses.

The Old Settlers had a complicated system of clans and moieties. Like most agriculturists, they were matrilineal, property and clan membership descending through the mother's line. A typical group of Old Settlers, the Mandan of the Missouri Valley, had seven clans, divided into two moieties, the "right" clans and the "left" clans. Mandan villages, usually built on high ground overlooking a river, consisted of big, strong houses as large as fifty feet in diameter and fifteen feet high. The clans of the two moieties occupied separate parts of the village. Several families would share a

single lodge, along with their dogs, and, later on, with their favorite horses as well.

It happened that the Mandan were light-skinned, as Indians go, and this gave rise to a bit of pseudoscientific mythology when they were discovered by white men in 1738. The explorers sent back word to their settlements that they had found the survivors of a "lost" expedition of white men who had come to the New World long before Columbus. "Their language is similar to Welsh," they reported, "and their faces are white."

The fancied resemblance of the Siouan Mandan language to Welsh touched off a flurry of scholarly activity. Someone uncovered the legend of a Welsh prince named Madoc, who supposedly sailed westward across the Atlantic in the year 1170. It was immediately concluded that the Mandan were Welshmen descended from Prince Madoc's expedition, and more than one lengthy volume was penned to prove the point. The fact that the Mandan language was not intelligible to real Welshmen who visited them in the service of the British Army was not considered important. After all, the argument ran, a language can change a great deal in six hundred years, especially if those who speak it are cut off in a remote land.

The Mandan were amused by the debate, but no real proof of their Welsh ancestry ever was put forth. In 1837, a smallpox epidemic nearly wiped them out, leaving only thirty-one survivors. Today there are about three hundred Mandan, but their alleged "Welsh" blood has been sadly diluted by intermarriage with the Aditsa and Arikara tribes.

IN THE YEAR 1598 something happened that eventually brought about a vast upheaval in the lives of the Old Settlers. Spanish colonists came to New Mexico, bringing with them great herds of sheep, goats, and horses. At first the Spanish, well aware of the danger of letting the Indians have horses, kept careful control over their steeds. Inevitably, though, a few horses escaped from the compounds each year and fled into the Plains. Eventually the Spanish relented and began to sell horses to the more remote Siouan tribes, though not to the Indians of New Mexico.

By the middle of the seventeenth century, the wild horses of the Plains, multiplying unchecked, had come to number in the thousands. The Indians had no name for them, and called them "mystery dogs" at first. For the horse, it was an ironic home-coming, since the first horses had evolved in the Americas millions of years before, only to die out along with the mammoth and mastodon in the days of Folsom Man. While Indians had been streaming into the Americas over the Siberian land bridge, horses had gone the other way, into Asia, and had become domesticated there. Now the Spanish had brought them back.

The Indians had no better use for them at the outset than to kill them for food. It was not long, though, before they saw how the Spanish used them for transportation. The first Indians who learned how to ride the "mystery dogs" at once acquired a tremendous advantage over their neighbors; they could ride out on terror raids covering hundreds of miles, invincible and frightening atop their majestic animals.

As much in self-defense as anything else, all the Plains tribes swiftly became horsemen. The horses were there for the taking, and it was only a matter of capturing them, breaking them, and learning how to ride them. No doubt in the beginning horsemanship seemed impossibly difficult. An engraving dating from the year 1700 shows an Indian *tied* to his horse. But within a few years they had mastered the knack of staying aboard, disdaining saddles, and using only a girth and a folded blanket. Within a generation the Indians excelled the whites as horsemen, performing such dazzling stunts as anchoring themselves to their horses by a loop of horsehair through which they thrust one foot, and leaning over their horses' sides to shoot arrows under their necks.

The way of life of the Old Settlers was dead within fifty years. For four centuries and more, the Indians of the Plains had been agriculturalists, but now they took to their horses and headed out to hunt the thronging buffalo.

Indians came from all sides. The Blackfeet, an Algonquian-speaking tribe from the eastern woodlands, moved into a broad territory ranging from Montana westward to the Rockies. The Cheyenne, the Arapaho, the Gros Ventre—all Algonquian tribes—also moved westward out of their cornfields. From west of the Plains came the Comanche, who spoke a language related to that of the Pueblo people of New Mexico, and the Kiowa, and the Shoshone. And, of course, there were the Siouan tribes, the Teton and Ponca and Omaha and all the rest.

Some came before the others, and could regard themselves as veterans of the Plains life. The Blackfeet were probably the first to take up the nomadic, buffalo-hunting existence. They were a sun-worshiping tribe who called themselves the "Siksika," after the black-dyed moccasins they wore, and who were really a confederation of three Algonquian tribes, the Siksika, the Bloods, and the Piegan. Then the Absaroke, whose name the English translated as "Crow," settled in the valley of the Yellowstone for a while before becoming hunters. The Mandan and the Arikara and the Hidatsa were also among the first to live the new life. Most of the Siouan tribes did not enter the Plains until the latter part of the eighteenth century, when they were driven westward out of their own country by Ojibwa armed with guns bought from the white men.

The Plains became a melting pot. Once the different tribes got there, they thrived; they took up basically similar ways of life, interchanged words from their languages, and developed a universal sign language that allowed a Siouan-speaking Indian to communicate easily with an Algonquian, with one who spoke a Uto-Aztecan language of the Southwest, or with one of the Athabascan-speaking Indians of the Northwest.

There was no longer any farming. The Plains were not suited for Indian agriculture, and in any event the buffalo provided food for all. Though some tribes, like the Mandan, raised a little corn even after the coming of horses to the Plains, most adopted a completely nomadic hunting way of life.

Individual hunting was frowned on. A lone hunter could do little against a herd of buffalo except, perhaps, stampede it into uncontrollable fury. Hunting became a collective responsibility. All the men of the tribe joined forces to surround the herd, cut off a manageable group of buffalo, and run them down. A horse could outrun a buffalo, so that a skilled Plains hunter could gallop alongside one of the unwieldy animals, choosing with

care the exact place to thrust his spear or discharge his
bow. (Even after flintlock guns came to the Plains
Indians in the nineteenth century, they still found it
more efficient to use their ancient weapons in the hunt.
Spears needed no reloading and were easier to handle
on horseback.)

The buffalo served many purposes. The fresh meat
was eaten, of course. Whatever could not be used at
once could be dried in the sun until it was hard as
bone; this jawbreaking stuff would keep for months
and could be put away to be eaten in winter when no
buffalo hunting was done. Some of the meat was made
into pemmican, an Indian delicacy that white men
never could learn to appreciate. The Indian women
made pemmican by pounding dried meat fine, and
mixing it with fat and dried berries.

Most of the meat, though, was eaten right away. The
Indians would gorge themselves on the fresh meat, dividing it so that everyone had all he could eat. The
tongue and liver were considered special treats, and
these were usually awarded to the man who had
actually killed the buffalo.

The skin of the buffalo served for cold-weather clothing, worn hairy-side-in. Scraped clean, buffalo hides
were used to make shields, bags, leather jackets and
leggings, moccasin soles, and a hundred other things.
Buffalo sinew became string and sewing thread.

The buffalo also provided housing for the Plains Indians. Since they had become nomads, following the
buffalo herds wherever they roamed, the Plains people

needed light, easily portable dwellings. The massive-walled sod huts that had served them in their Old Settler days as farmers would not answer the new needs.

They adapted the tipi of the eastern woodlands Algonquians to their own purposes. In the East, tipis were made of birch bark over a framework of poles, but there was no birch on the Plains. Buffalo hide served instead. Ten to twelve hides, taken in springtime from buffalo who had just shed their winter coats, were sewn together in a roughly semicircular strip and laid on the ground. Three or four foundation poles of cedar or lodgepole pine were placed over the hides for measurement, and then were tied together at one end and set upright. Other poles were added, until there were twenty or twenty-five of them, about twenty feet high. The last poles to go up had the buffalo-hide cover attached to them, and it was then lashed into place. It took no more than five minutes for a few skilled Indians to erect a tipi.

At first, in the spring, the tipis were clean and white, and they were decorated with painted animal images or sometimes with quills and beads. As the year went along, smoke from the fire within gradually darkened the hides until, by the time a tipi was old and ready to be discarded the following April, it would be almost black.

Most of these tasks—drying meat, dressing skins, making pemmican, raising or dismantling tipis—fell to the lot of the women; but the Plains women did not play as important a role in their society as did women among the farming Indians. Here there were no fields and houses to be owned, no "real estate." So, whereas in the more settled tribes the women had been the owners and the inheritors, out in the open Plains they settled into a life of quiet drudgery without power or real tribal responsibilities. It was the men who did the food-providing, the men who ruled the tribes, the men who lived the dashing, glamorous life of free horsemen. With some exceptions, descent was traced through the father's line, and it was around the doings of the men that the whole life of the tribe revolved.

The men had plenty of free time. They did most of their hunting in the summer, and the buffalo were so numerous that it was no problem to bring back enough food to last through the year. The rest of the time, the warriors devoted themselves to the leisurely joys of manhood: games, contests, dances, horsemanship, and a great many secret societies where, safe from the dreary drudgery of everyday chores, they could boast to one another of their prowess in the hunt and in battle.

Prestige was everything. The Plains Indians were ambitious, competitive, fiercely proud of their accomplishments. They saw life in a dramatic, colorful way. The Blackfoot secret society of Crazy Dogs had a war song that typified the Plains attitude toward life:

> It is bad to live to be old.
> Better to die young
> Fighting bravely in battle.

The life of a Plains brave was a constant struggle to

achieve status. Just as modern "status seekers" strive to possess fine cars, imposing houses, expensive jewelry, and other luxury items, so did the status seekers of the Plains exert themselves to impress their companions with their importance.

The Plains equivalent of the Cadillac was the horse. The more horses a man owned, the more powerful he was, and so fortune was counted in horses. A man needed a strong horse for his own personal use, of course, but that was not all. He needed many others, to use as gifts, to purchase wives, and simply to show off. No Plains Indian could count himself as important if he had less than fifty horses. Some plutocrats owned two hundred or more. The horse raid, in which Indians of one tribe swooped down to steal the horses of another, was the most important activity of the Plains warriors.

Boys were taught this way of life as soon as they were old enough to walk. War and hunting were the means of showing prowess on the Plains, and even toddlers went out to kill rabbits, and, when they were a little older, buffalo calves.

A man took pride in the exploits of his sons. Each step on a boy's road to manhood was marked by a great feast. His father would summon as many guests as he could afford to entertain. Naturally, the bigger and costlier the feast, the greater was the father's prestige.

A brave could not marry until he had established himself as a man of valor by winning war honors and acquiring horses. It was necessary for a would-be husband to make a handsome gift to the brother of his beloved, and often a man would reach his late twenties before he could afford the gift and the feast that had to follow it. Later, a man in the prime of his life might "throw away" a wife, divorcing her at a feast just to show how great his wealth was. Men were allowed to take as many wives as they could afford. A man usually married all his wife's sisters, and if he died, his brother or cousin was required to take them into his family.

The war societies were the core of a man's existence. We have seen how, among nearly all the Indians of the East, war was a vital part of life, a way of proving manhood. Out on the Plains, it was even more so. War was a way of life.

Each tribe had a number of secret societies, some more important than others. Their general role in the tribe was remarkably like that of the fraternity in college. Each society had its own initiation customs, its own symbols, its own sense of exclusiveness. From membership in such a group a man drew a heightened sense of his own importance.

A boy in his teens would buy his way into the lowest-ranked society by presenting gifts to the members, particularly to one member who would agree to sponsor him. Then he would spend the rest of his life striving to move up the ladder into the more important societies, buying his way in at each step. Mere wealth, however, was not enough; a man had to have a reputation for valor as well. But among the Plains Indians it usually happened that the most valorous were also the wealthiest, since wealth could be obtained only through exploits of courage.

There might be a dozen or more of these societies in some of the bigger tribes. Among the Mandan and the Hidatsa there were eleven secret societies, whose names were, in rising order of prestige, Notched Stick, Stone Hammer, Crazy Dogs, Lumpwood, Kit-Foxes, Little Dogs, Dogs, Half-Shaved Heads, Black Mouths, Bulls, and Ravens. A man who had passed through the entire series from lowest to highest was rewarded with the strange title of "Stinking Ear."

A man won prestige on the battlefield by performing certain clearly defined actions. The most highly valued was to touch a live enemy on the battlefield with a special stick. This meant getting within arm's length of him—a much more dangerous feat than fighting at a distance with bow and arrow. The act of touching an enemy was known as "counting coup," from the French word *coup*, a blow. When counting coup, the Plains brave had to cry out loudly, "I perform the brave deed of counting coup upon this man who is brave among our enemies."

Slightly less valuable was the act of counting coup on a dead enemy surrounded by his live and fighting comrades. Entering an enemy camp to steal a horse also entitled a man to count coup. Killing an enemy at a distance, or scalping a dead or dying man, were considered relatively minor accomplishments.

When a Plains warrior returned to the camp, he would boast of his deeds. This boasting was a ritualized institution performed according to highly involved rules. A man could boast only of deeds that others had witnessed, for woe betide a lying braggart!

Dakota honor feathers for coups in battle; Omaha warriors' bonnets

Touching an enemy with the coupstick allowed a brave to wear an upright feather in his bonnet. A backward-sloping feather indicated a wound received honorably in battle. A round mark on the feather meant that a man had killed his opponent, and a red feather with a notch in it symbolized the taking of an enemy scalp. The performance of ten brave deeds in battle entitled a man to wear the big feather war bonnet so familiar in Western movies. The greatest warriors wore bonnets with two long streamers of eagle feathers down their backs.

In religion, too, the men competed with each other to show their endurance and ability to withstand hardship. Like many Indians, those of the Plains laid great store by visions, and each young man had to go off alone to fast for days until a dream came to him from the spirit world. But Plains religion went on to include other features verging on self-torture.

Every year, Plains tribes from all over would gather for a rite called the "Sun Dance." Sun worship is common to agricultural peoples, and the Plains Indians brought their Sun religion with them when they left their old life. At Sun Dance time, feasting and games were the order of the day for the women and old people, but the young warriors had special obligations.

They would dance around a central pole for hours and sometimes days on end without a break, capering wildly to, and then past, the point of exhaustion. To make their ordeal all the more exacting, sharp sticks would be thrust under the skin of their backs and chests. These sticks would be tied by ropes to the center pole and, as a result of the wild dancing, would be jerked from their skins. Blood flowed freely, but it was forbidden to show any sign of pain. Probably in the ecstasy of their dance the braves did not actually feel the pain. The scars of the Sun Dance were proudly displayed afterward.

Another means of winning prestige was through the feast. Plains Indians constantly threw feasts for their friends, and vied with each other in generosity. The most ambitious of the Sioux held Give Away Feasts, to which whole tribes were invited. During a long Give Away Feast a man might distribute not only meat but clothing, horses, bows and arrows, buffalo robes—and even wives! The greatest honor of all went to the man who gave away so much that he left himself all but pauperized. Of course, he did not stay poor for long, because his example would lead others of his tribe to throw Give Away Feasts of their own and much of his property would soon return to him. (We shall en-

Plains Indians warriors performing Sun Dance

counter this kind of feasting again when we turn to the Indians of the Pacific Northwest, among whom it assumed fantastic proportions.)

It was a strenuous and taxing life. As happens in every society, there were a few men who for reasons of temperament or physical weakness were unable to compete with the others. Such men did not ride or hunt, and they had to wear women's clothes and perform women's chores. But they were not treated with contempt; they had religious duties to perform that won them a place of sorts in the tribe.

THE WHITE MAN did not completely exterminate the Plains Indians as he did those of New England, or drive them to another part of the country as he did the Choctaw and Cherokee. What he did was far worse, in a way: he left them on their lands, but destroyed their way of life.

The battle between the white man and the Plains Indian lasted through most of the nineteenth century, and its details are well known through fiction and motion pictures. Indian chiefs like Red Cloud and Sitting Bull, who led the resistance against the invaders, have become heroes of legendary degree.

The worst warfare came in the 1870's, when veterans of the Civil War flocked westward to begin new lives as farmers and ranchers on the Great Plains. The Indians resisted, and massacre followed bloody massacre until the strength and spirit of the Plainsmen were broken. There were the usual treaties with the survivors, and the treaties were broken in the usual way. Eventually, the many thousands of Plains Indians who were left were penned up in reservations, forbidden to hunt or to dance their dances, which seemed barbaric and shocking to the white men.

Government representatives tried to teach the Plains Indians how to farm. But they had had three hundred years of warrior's freedom. Farming was women's work, and they would have none of it. They clustered glumly on their reservations, consoling themselves with liquor and taking up new dancing religions, which the white men suppressed.

"The Indians won't work," people said. To which the Plains people answered, in the words of one Comanche, "The earth is my mother. Do you give me an iron plow to wound my mother's breast? Shall I take a scythe and cut my mother's hair?" Starvation and poverty, sickness and drunkenness swept through these unhappy Indians. By the end of the nineteenth century, the settlers from the East had just about wiped out the once uncountable buffalo herds, and the Sioux and the other Plains Indians knew at last that there could be no going back to their old hunting existence.

For generations, the conquerors stubbornly tried to turn these warriors into farmers. It could not work, and it did not work. A large Indian population—more than thirty-five thousand—seemed doomed to waste away in idleness and misery. Today, though, the government is encouraging the Plains Indians to become cattlemen and ranchers. Where once they hunted buffalo, today they raise cattle in community herds, and they are at last winning their way back to self-respect.

Some of them earn their livings in another way. They live in Los Angeles and act in motion pictures. As skillful on horseback as ever, they deck themselves out in feathers and war paint, and relive the life of the old days when a hundred tribes roamed the prairies. Do they ever stop really to hearken back to the Sun Dance and the secret societies, the old free life of the Plains? Probably not. Probably, as they cash their movie-studio paychecks, they prefer not to think that in another time they could have lived in tipis on the Plains, riding out on powerful steeds to strike down the buffalo and feast joyfully on his inexhaustible meat.

10

NORTH OF
THE BORDER

A BOUNDARY IS A MAN-MADE THING. IT STRETCHES from here to there, invisible but terribly important to those who draw it. The boundary between the United States and Canada is a white man's line. The Indians did not draw that line, and it was no part of their world. Some Indian tribes dwelt only on the Canadian side of the line, while others, heedless of the white man's boundaries, lived on both sides and found their territories split by a political situation they neither created nor understood.

In the East, for instance, the Mohawk lived in upper New York State and also on the far side of the St. Lawrence River, in Canada. That geographical accident has caused no end of complications for them. Today, the St. Regis Mohawk Reservation is partly in Canada, partly in the United States. Half the people of the reservation are American citizens, half Canadians. The Canadian Government forbids the American Mohawk to seek work on the other side of the line, although Canadian Mohawk are free to come to the United States for jobs. This has set the reservation in conflict, and there have been cases in which Indians crossing the line to take work on the other side have been murdered. Yet they are all Mohawk, all Iroquois, divided by an invisible line that can set a man's hand against his brother.

Once there were no such artificial divisions, and Indians crossed as they pleased. Thus many of the Indians of Canada are tribes we have already met. More Blackfeet lived north of the border than below it. So, too, with the Ojibwa or Chippeway, who hunted and fished in what is now the Province of Manitoba with its thousands of lakes. In the East, there were many Iroquoian Indians in Canada, mostly Huron and members of the so-called Neutral Nation. Of the Iroquois proper, the Five Nations, only the Mohawk lived north of the line.

The rest of Canada was occupied by representatives of three big language groups. In the extreme north lived (and still live) the Eskimo, fascinating and important, but not considered Indians. Flat-faced and stocky, the Eskimo show pure Mongoloid traits that set them apart physically from Indians, though like all the original inhabitants of the Americas they most likely came from Asia.

The Indians proper of Canada fall into two families. In the East are Algonquians; in the West, Athabascans. Hudson Bay is the dividing line—a natural boundary, no man-made line this time. The only Canadian Indians who fitted into neither category were the extinct Beothuk of Newfoundland. They died out long ago, and little is known of them except their habit of coloring their skins with red ochre. (As we mentioned, it was a habit which probably led John Cabot, in 1497, to give the natives of North America the misleading label of "red men.")

There was little or no farming anywhere in Canada. Today, with modern agricultural methods, the farmlands of Canada yield rich harvests of grain, but the Indians were unable to cope with Canada's short summers and chilly climate. Corn, the prime crop of the agricultural Indians, was not suitable for cultivation in Canada.

In any case they had no reason to struggle against the climate, not while Canada's forests and lakes abounded with wild life. Hunting and fishing provided them with food, and they supplemented their diet by eating the berries, roots, and wild vegetables gathered by the women.

The Algonquians of eastern Canada were great trappers. These tribes included the Algonquins (who gave their name to the entire language group), the Montagnais, the Cree, the Salteaux, the Naskapi, and others. Skilled with snare and trap, they preyed on the thronging beaver population of the streams and brooks. Beaver meat was taken as food; the handsome pelts were made into clothing, and the surplus fur was traded to tribes to the south in return for corn, tobacco, and other goods not produced in Canada. These Algonquian

Indians thus became experienced tradesmen long before the white explorers arrived. The name of one tribe, the Ottawa, actually means "He buys." When the French and Dutch came to the New World, the Algonquians found their business increasing. The Dutch used the Iroquois as middlemen; Iroquois "businessmen" bought furs from the Algonquians for produce, and sold them to the Dutch for guns. The Montagnais, the Algonquin, and the Iroquoian Huron did so much business with the French settlers of Canada that they became known as "French Indians." The French sold guns to them, too, but insisted on selling them only to Christian Indians. Thousands of "French Indians" immediately accepted Christianity and happily traded furs for guns. Whether they practiced Christian rites when safely out of sight of the French priests is a matter of more than a little doubt.

So far as religion and customs went, these Algonquians of eastern Canada were not at all different from their cousins south of the line. They had the same festivals, the same religious outlook, the same way of life. The Cree, an Algonquian tribe of northeast Canada, were much like the Ojibwa, while the Algonquin and Montagnais generally followed the same patterns as the Algonquians of New England and the Middle Atlantic coast. They had no pottery, used bark for vessels and canoes, lived in wigwams or tipis, fashioned their snares and tents in the same way, employed snowshoes or toboggans for transportation in winter.

West of Hudson Bay we come to a different sort of Indians. They were hunters and fishers also, of course, but culturally different from the Algonquians of the East. These are the Athabascan-speaking Indians.

The Athabascan language group was extremely widespread. It began in the far Northwest, at the edge of the Eskimo world, and extended eastward to Hudson Bay and southward almost to the Great Plains, where it met a projecting arm of Algonquian-speaking Indians. There was also an island of Athabascan speech in the American Southwest—the Apache and Navaho Indians—several thousand miles from the main Athabascan territory.

A small fringe of western Canada did not belong to this Athabascan region. Along the coastal strip were Indians who spoke languages that do not fit into any of the six great categories—the Salishan, the Kutenai, the Wakashan, and others who will have a chapter of their own later on. Inland began the Athabascan territory.

One interesting Athabascan tribe was that of the Carrier Indians, who acquired their name from the grotesque custom of requiring widows to carry on their backs, during a three-year mourning period, baskets containing the charred remains of their husbands' bones. The Carrier Indians lived west of the Rockies, cut off by that chain from the main body of the Athabascan-speaking Indians, and were influenced in many ways by the inhabitants of the coastal strip. One custom of the Pacific Coast that has already been men-

tioned was the giving of elaborate feasts that often bankrupted the giver, and the Carrier people adopted this idea. An oddity of Carrier life was the habit they had of dropping their own names at the birth of their first children, and becoming known thereafter as "The father (or mother) of so-and-so."

The Carrier Indians had some unusual customs, but their basic way of life was characteristic of that of all the Athabascans. They were hunters and fishers. In the spring they fished for salmon which crowded every river west of the Rockies as they swam upstream to spawn. Summer was the time for trapping small animals in the foothills; in the fall the Carrier came down to the coast to trade. In early winter, with snow slowing the big animals and making their tracks visible, the Carrier hunted caribou. Then they settled down in their houses of logs or upright planks to wait the winter out, living off dried meat and roots until the fishing season began.

In the area east of the Rockies and west of Hudson Bay lived a large number of Athabascan tribes known by the general name of the Dené, a word derived from their own name for themselves, *Tinneh,* which simply means The People.

They were hunters, and still are, since many Indian tribes live almost unchanged in Canada's relatively un-developed northern reaches. Their chief target was the caribou, or reindeer, that bulky, hairy-muzzled, clumsy-looking creature whose great antlers adorn so many fireplaces. The caribou was to the Dené what the buffalo was for the Indians of the Plains. Indeed, some of the southern Dené tribes, such as the Sarcee, shared all the customs and viewpoints of the Plains Indians, except that one hunted caribou and the other buffalo.

Caribou are peaceful, vegetation-browsing creatures which move in large herds, migrating northward in late spring and returning in autumn. The Dené hunted them on foot, tracking them on snowshoes in the early winter or converging on them during their spring migration. The method was the age-old one of stam-peding the animals, either over cliffs or into dead-end enclosures where they could be speared. When pos-sible, the caribou would be driven into rivers and lakes, where spearsmen could follow them in fast-moving canoes. Killing caribou was never really difficult, and when the Indians obtained guns from the white man, they nearly slaughtered their entire food supply, thining the herds sharply.

The caribou move fast when migrating, and the hunters who followed them had to keep pace. It was impossible to haul the entire kill from one place to another, so the Dené built storage caches, elevated platforms or subterranean enclosures, where they could leave their meat to dry or freeze. Each day they would dress their kill, cache it, and then move on, returning later to collect their stores. As in other Indian regions where more meat could be obtained than could immediately be eaten, the Dené made long-lasting pemmican by pounding meat and berries and sealing the result in melted fat.

Moose, elk, deer, and, where they ranged, buffalo were other Dené victims. They did some fishing and trapping of small game.

Physically, the Dené resembled their Eskimo neighbors to the north more than they did the Algonquians to the east and south. They had strong Mongoloid characteristics, indicating that they were relative newcomers to the Americas. Their noses were straight but small, their eyes had a visible slant, and their skins tended toward the yellowish brown. They were round-headed, stocky, and usually did not live long lives.

Since they were nomads, they had no very complicated social organization. They had tribal units, but no confederations or leagues. There was a clan system, with descent through the female line. Children belonged to their mother's clan, and their father was not even considered to be related to them. Thus a man could marry his father's younger sister or his father's niece without causing any comment. (But he could not, of course, marry any of his mother's relatives, since they were of his own clan.)

A Dené man could have many wives. The process of acquiring them was simple. A man could buy a wife from her mother for a few caribou hides. If he happened to take a fancy to another man's wife, he had the right to challenge the other husband to a wrestling match. The winner got the woman. Strong men thus had the most wives—a sensible enough system, since in that rugged hunting society the strongest men were best suited to provide for women.

A woman's life among the Dené was nothing enviable. In all Dené tribes the women worked endlessly; and among some, such as the Kutchin, a wife was regarded as nothing more than a slave. Kutchin wives dragged sleds, carried burdens, built dwellings. When a man cached meat at the hunting grounds, he sent his wife out to haul it home. (Though, interestingly, the Kutchin men did the cooking when the meat got home!) So harsh was the lot of a woman that some Dené mothers would kill girl children at birth to spare them from a life of toil. Others who got short shrift among these hunters were the old and feeble, who generally were murdered or abandoned in the woods when they became too much of a burden.

The loosely organized Dené tribes had chiefs, but

their powers were limited and they could be over-
thrown at any time by challengers, quite different
from the Iroquois or Muskhogean arrangement where
the right to rule was hereditary and not subject to
challenge except on grounds of incompetence. The
real power in a Dené tribe was held by the shaman,
or medicine man. Superstitious and fearful, the Athabascans cowered before their shamans (who were
usually crafty men unsuited for the life of a hunter).
A shaman could, it was believed, spoil a hunter's luck,
bring illness or bad weather, and even kill by magic.
So long as his own luck held out and he continued to
make his tribesmen believe he had magical powers, a
shaman could be virtually a dictator in his tribe.

The Dené learned from many sides. From the Es-

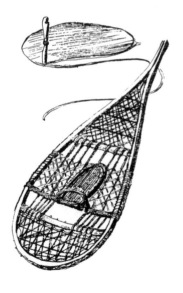

kimo, with whom they traded, they learned how to make clothing out of hides. Both men and women wore trousers, hooded shirts that hung loosely, and mittens. In cold weather, the Dené wore two shirts: one next to the skin, fur-side-in, and another over it, fur-side-out.

From the Algonquians, the Dené learned how to make canoes, tipis, and wigwams. Birch was available only in southern Canada, but beyond the birch range the Dené used the bark of spruce or cedar for their canoes. They also made cooking vessels out of spruce bark, boiling their food by dropping hot stones into water. Their tipis, and the wigwams in which they spent the winter, were covered with hides for greater warmth.

The Athabascans were not only borrowers but teachers, to some extent. They made the finest snowshoes in North America, and probably brought the idea to the Algonquians. They were expert, too, in porcupine-quill ornamentation and in weaving nets and snares. Some Dené tribes mined copper and sold it to other Indian groups; they made only slight use of it themselves.

An important Dené product was babiche, leather string cut from the hides of deer, moose, or caribou. Southern tribes made their string from plants, but the Dené did not have such plants available. They made babiche by pulling a hide along a sharp blade, and they became expert at cutting it into very thin strips. Babiche made from deer or moose hides would shrink when wet, and so could be used for tight lashings. Caribou-hide babiche hardly shrank at all, which made it ideal for the webbing of snowshoes.

There were no horses in Athabascan country. Dog-power provided the chief means of transportation, and when no dogs were available women generally did the hauling. The usual vehicle was the toboggan, made of thin boards of spruce lashed together with babiche.

Life among these Athabascan Indians of Canada was primitive, rugged, and brief. Less is known of them than of almost any other group of Indians, even though their culture has survived on into our century. For every anthropologist who has gone into Dené country to study them, a hundred or more have gone to the pueblos of the Southwest or to the colorful villages of the Pacific Northwest.

One reason for this neglect, it would seem, is the simplicity of these northern woodsmen. Lacking any real culture of their own, easily swayed by the ways of their neighbors, they offer few rewards for the student, and few have ventured into their bleak homeland. Athabascans still hunt and fish in the big woods, moving in little nomadic bands, living as they have lived for hundreds of years. Thanks to the white man's weapons, they have seriously cut down their own food supply, the caribou. And, with the aid of the white man's diseases and his whiskey, they have managed almost to wipe themselves out as well.

There are still a few left, however, in Canada's back yard. Most of North America's Indians collided violently with the white man and suffered for it. The Dené have simply been ignored.

11

CLIFF DWELLERS
AND DESERT FOLK

FROM THE BLEAK CANADIAN WOODS, WE TURN TO A part of North America where winter hardly comes at all, where the kindly sun smiles down almost every day of the year. And leaving some of America's simplest Indians, we come to a group whose highly developed and advanced culture can trace its ancestry back across thousands of years.

These are the Pueblo Indians of the Southwest—the Hopi, the Zuni, and their cousins, tillers of the soil and builders of remarkable houses. They live where Indians have lived since the days of Folsom Man, and their dwelling places are the oldest continuously inhabited villages in the Americas.

The beginning of their story is lost in time's mists. Archaeologists have uncovered traces of farming peoples in the Southwest dating back five thousand years or more. We mentioned, in Chapter Three, the Cochise people who, though they did not raise vegetables, understood how to grind them for food. The skill was the beginning of agriculture in North America, possibly ten thousand years ago. We noted, too, the discovery of cultivated corn in Bat Cave, New Mexico, with a radiocarbon age of fifty-six hundred years.

Arizona and New Mexico were the central sites of this farming culture, though it reached out into what is now Nevada, Utah, and Colorado—and across the border into Mexico, too. What happened in Mexico is beyond the scope of this book, for there is not enough room even to start discussing the complex Aztec, Toltec, and Maya cultures and their ancestors. The Indians of Arizona and New Mexico never attained the heights of the empire builders of Mexico, but their civilization was impressive in its own right.

Actually there were several Southwestern civilizations, related but not identical. The ancestor of them all was the Cochise civilization, those long-ago grinders of seeds and nuts. Probably the Cochise people at first were seminomadic, wandering through the Southwest in search of dependable supplies of food. But during the thousands of years that followed the time when they first learned how to grind seeds, the climate of the Southwest changed. It became arid. Lake Cochise dried up altogether. Fertile forest land turned into desert.

It was no longer so easy to live by gathering seeds, and the Indians, as desert people, had to raise their own food and tend it with loving care. The old Cochise people gave way to two daughter-cultures; they were no longer food-gatherers but farmers. We call these two new cultures, which probably crystallized about 100 B.C., the Hohokam and the Mogollon—Pima Indian names meaning "The Old Ones."

The Hohokam lived in the river valleys of southern Arizona, along the Gila and Salt rivers, not far from present-day Phoenix. The closely related Mogollon lived to the east, in southern New Mexico.

Corn, beans, and squash were their important crops. Despite the dryness of their territory, they could usually depend on six weeks of rain beginning in midsummer, and so long as the rains came they could grow corn. Naturally, the religion of the Southwest revolved around the need for rain. The Rain Dances of the present-day Indians of the Southwest must go back, in one form or another, to the Mogollon-Hohokam days of two thousand years ago.

Rain alone was not enough. In the torrid, cactus-studded plain, the thirsty earth drank the summer rain eagerly and dryness would return. The Hohokam learned to build irrigation ditches to tap the water of the Gila River. No other Indian engineering accomplishments of North America equal these Hohokam canals. The earliest ones, built perhaps about A.D. 300, were little more than shallow ditches scraped out with stone hoes, but between A.D. 700 and A.D. 1000 the Hohokam built a series of mighty canals, twenty-five feet wide and fifteen feet deep, some of which ran for sixteen miles. Thousands of acres were under irrigation; one Hohokam canal network alone totaled one hundred fifty miles. These were solidly built canals, which remained in use long after the Hohokam themselves had disappeared. As late as the eighteenth century, a Spanish priest in Arizona wrote of "a very large canal, still open for the distance of some two leagues . . . it appears to have supplied a city with water, and irrigated many leagues of the rich country of those beautiful plains."

These hard-working desert dwellers had no poles or bark, and so built their homes in earth-covered pits in the ground. They wove tough vegetable fibers into clothing, made sandals from straw, blankets from twined-together ropes of rabbitskin. They used a simple loom for their weaving, unlike any of the other North American Indians of their time, and made respectable-looking pottery. Indian pottery was always made out of coils of clay arranged one atop the other and smoothed into shape; the potter's wheel was never invented anywhere in the New World, not even among the sophisticated Peruvians whose remarkable pottery was so skillfully made and so attractive.

There was contact between the Hohokam and the Indian tribes of Mexico. We know this because the same types of art work are found throughout the whole area from Mexico City northward: clay figurines of snakes and birds, mosaic work in turquoise, copper ornaments.

About A.D. 1200 other desert tribes began to move into Hohokam-Mogollon territory. It was not really an invasion, but more of a peaceful mingling, since these farming peoples of the Southwest have never been warlike. The nature of Hohokam and Mogollon life began to change. No more canals were built. Craftsmanship declined. Exactly what happened we are not sure, but it seems likely that invaders were coming down out of the North, the Navaho and Apache, who spoke Athabascan languages pointing to their Canadian origin. As the peaceful desert dwellers moved about to escape these raiders, more of them gathered in Hohokam country. The old Hohokam farmers mingled with the simpler seed-gathering folk who took refuge with them, and gradually the Hohokam way of life died out. There was one last flourish of Hohokam engineering skill about A.D. 1300, when the people living along the Gila River began to build massive "skyscrapers," three and four stories high, out of adobe brick.

By the time the Spanish came to Arizona and New Mexico, the Indians living in the southern desert were a much simpler folk than the old Hohokam and Mogollon. These remnants are known as the Pima and Papago. "Pima," in the desert language, simply means "I don't know," which is the answer they gave to every question the Spanish asked. "Papago" means "The Bean People," after their chief crop.

Peaceful and industrious, they raised corn and beans and pumpkins in the dry climate, and gathered cactus from the plains, eating the fruit and stems, using the thorns as needles, and making a kind of cider from the plant's fluids. In temperament the Pima and the Papago were the direct opposite of the Indians of the Plains. They did not long to be important. They had no hunger for power. There were no warriors, no chiefs, no confederacies. Each village was headed by a "big man" chosen for his wisdom; he and four assistants led the prayers for rain, settled the occasional disputes in the village, and presided over the village councils. There was a halfhearted clan system, with descent through the father's line, but it never exerted much influence on the lives of the people, who merely were bound to marry someone from another village.

There comes a time when even the most peace-loving people must fight, if only to defend their homelands. The Pima and Papago, neighbors to the warlike Navaho and Apache, were no exceptions. War always struck them as a grim, horrifying necessity. They hated it. They fought only to defend themselves, and in the hope that displaying bravery would bring rain. To them war was insanity. A typical Pima war speech shows how totally unbelligerent these Indians were:

"You may think this over, my relatives. The taking of life brings serious thoughts of the waste. The celebration of victory may become unpleasantly riotous."

The Pima and Papago would go forth against the enemy like reluctant draftees who fight because they know it is their duty. Only one or two men in a raiding band would actually kill, leaders known as "the hard man" or "the angry man." When the warriors returned from the raid, those who had killed would walk apart from the others, their faces blackened. They were unclean, and contact with them would contaminate the others.

While the villagers danced to welcome the warriors

home, the killers, far from being greeted as victorious heroes, had to remain in lonely quarantine for sixteen days, praying for purification. They could not speak, could eat only certain foods, were not permitted to look at the sun or at a fire. Old men brought them their scanty rations, and addressed them in this fashion:

> Verily, who desires this?
> Did not you desire it?
> Then you must endure many hardships.

When they were not called upon to make war, these desert Indians had their rain-making festivals to occupy them, and the worship of animal spirits and of the creator-god, known as Elder Brother. Priests led these activities, and also served as doctors. Now and then, too many of a priest's patients would die, and he would be accused of witchcraft and publicly clubbed to death, almost the only dark aspect of life among these sunny people.

WHILE THE COCHISE CULTURE was turning into Hohokam and Mogollon in the South, a different kind of civilization was developing on the dry plateau that cuts diagonally across upper Arizona and New Mexico. It arose in the high, rocky country where today the four corners of Utah, Colorado, New Mexico, and Arizona meet. We call this civilization the Anasazi, from the Navaho word meaning "Ancient Ones."

The Anasazi were related to the Hohokam and Mogollon, and probably both were descended from the

Cochise people. In the North, though, farming was a later arrival. Not until about A.D. 200 did the Anasazi begin to raise corn. It was even later that they took up pottery.

The earliest Anasazi culture is known as the Basketmaker Culture. The Basketmakers, as the name implies, were expert weavers, and in the dry climate of the Southwest much of their handiwork survived to be found by archaeologists two thousand years later. Some of the baskets were made of yucca fibers, others of wooden splints or shredded roots. All were remarkable works of craftsmanship. The Basketmakers stored their

Pueblo women decorating pottery and grinding corn on stone mortar in front of "apartment houses"

seeds and dried vegetables in baskets, and also, by making them watertight with clay daubs, used them for cooking vessels, into which they threw hot stones to make the water boil.

At first the Basketmakers lived in pit houses, as in the South. They dug down several feet and threw up lean-tos of brush-covered poles. Nearby caves served for the storage of baskets of seeds.

Century by century, the Basketmakers learned to improve their ways of doing things. They bred small corn, with ears only four inches long, and though they were not able to build irrigation canals as did the Hohokam, they managed somehow to keep their small cornfields watered. They learned how to make pottery, crude at first but better after a while. They improved their pit houses by lining them with stones and plastering the lean-tos with mud.

About A.D. 700 or A.D. 800, the Basketmakers stopped

living in pit houses altogether. They began to build dwellings completely aboveground, first of mud and logs, and later of stone. They would build these houses in clusters, arranged in semicircular arcs. Clans lived together. A mother, her daughters, and their husbands all built houses in the same part of the village. The old pit houses were still used for storage and for religious purposes.

The years between A.D. 900 and A.D. 1300 were the great years of the Anasazi culture. We do not call them Basketmakers at this stage, because the old basketwork had largely been replaced by excellent pottery. The new phase of Anasazi culture is called "Pueblo," the Spanish word for "town."

And towns they were, these dwellings of the Anasazi. Through a gradual process of evolution, the separate mud or stone houses joined together, first one clan choosing to live in adjoining rooms, then whole villages coming together so that all lived in the same large house of many rooms and many stories. In the valley of the Chaco Canyon, New Mexico, these giant communal houses attained their peak of development. The most famous of the dozen houses there is Pueblo Bonito, with five stories rising in setback terraces. Pueblo Bonito, with more than eight hundred rooms, covered more than three acres. Tree-ring dates taken from timbers tell us that it was nearly one hundred fifty years in the building, from A.D. 919 to A.D. 1067. It was the world's largest "apartment house" until 1882, when a bigger one was built in New York.

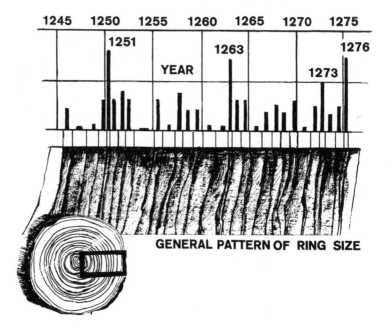

Long vertical bars on tree ring chart of charred beam from Pueblo Bonito indicate years of severe drought in which rings were close together. Cross checks with other samples establish years wood from beam was alive.

Those were the great days of the Anasazi. Magnificent pueblos, made of sandstone slabs artfully fitted together, rose along every important river. From the Anasazi kilns streamed attractive, sturdy pottery, and the women at their looms produced gaily colored blankets. The fields yielded corn, squash, beans, cotton, and tobacco. Even in the imposing "apartment houses," the old pit houses were retained, circular rooms below ground level, entered through the roof. These were religious centers for the men, chapels known as "kivas." Prayer was vital to these people, dependent as they were on the mercies of the rain-gods.

The rain-gods ultimately withheld their bounty, and the Pueblo people suffered. Their civilization shriveled. The thirteenth century saw many of the great pueblos abandoned. The evidence of the tree rings tells of a terrible drought from 1276 to 1299, a quarter of a century virtually without rain! Were prayers neglected? Were the gods angry?

Drought was not the only Pueblo problem. While dust devils swirled over their parched fields, fierce invaders entered their land from the North—the Apache, the Navaho. The peaceful Pueblo people had not planned on invasion. Pueblo Bonito was innocently built in the middle of a plain, vulnerable to attack on all sides.

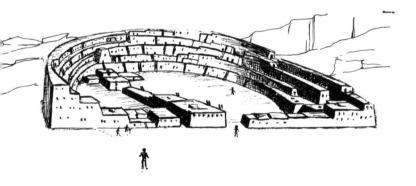

Archaeologists' reconstruction of Pueblo Bonito

Many of the Pueblo Indians moved away, southward into the Rio Grande Valley. Those who remained built themselves a new kind of house, carved in recesses of inaccessible cliffs. There, at least, they were safe from the nomads, and they farmed as best they could on the flat-topped mesas, always harried by drought. Finally they, too, moved southward.

The Pueblo refugees came into the country of the Hohokam, who were also in a time of decline. For a century or more, the Anasazi and Hohokam lived side by side, each practicing their own customs, Anasazi buring their dead, Hohokam cremating theirs; Anasazi smoking pipes, Hohokam cigarettes, and so on. Then the Pueblo Indians moved on again, into western New Mexico and southward into Mexico itself. They built new cities of stone, plastering up the chinks of their buildings with adobe. The houses adjoined each other, and often were two and three stories high, but none of the new villages approached the size of Pueblo Bonito and the other great buildings of the past. There the Pueblos farmed, and prayed for rain, and lived as they had long been living.

There the Spanish found them, when they came to settle in New Mexico at the beginning of the seventeenth century. The newcomers preached Christianity to the Pueblo people, and taught them to grow wheat and peaches and peppers, but they did not really change them in any significant way. White man and red lived side by side, fairly peacefully (except for such violent interludes as the Pueblo Rebellion of 1680, when a sudden uprising drove the Spaniards out for a dozen years). The Pueblo way of life remained intact down to our own time. The stolid, peaceful Indians simply shrugged off the presence of white men and went on living as they had always lived. Only in the last twenty years has the world of the automobile and the television set made any real inroads into Pueblo existence. As a result, we know more about Pueblo beliefs and attitudes than we do about any other North American Indians. Anthropologists have been able to study them "in the flesh," instead of piecing together a network of conjecture out of traditions, legends, and fragmentary archaeological evidence.

THE PUEBLO PEOPLE who have been observed most closely are the Hopi and Zuni, desert dwellers of New Mexico and eastern Arizona. Their villages are of differing kinds. Some, in the high mesa country, are built of stone. Others, in the lowlands, are made of adobe "bricks." The architectural style is similar, whatever the building material—square, flat-topped houses several stories high, each village bristling with spidery ladders that lead to the upper stories.

The Hopi have six towns on three high mesas in Arizona. A seventh Hopi town is shared with a related people, the Tewa, who have lived with the Hopi for two centuries. In their own language, the Hopi are the *Hopitu*—"Peaceful Ones." Good-natured and easygoing, they abhorred war as much as the Pima, and would fight only when driven to desperation by the

Apache and Navaho. So peaceful and noncompetitive
were the Hopi (and it must be remembered that the
use of past tense is only partly accurate, since many
of them still live in the old way) that they cared little
for sports or gambling, unlike almost all the other
Indians of North America.

They did not look much like other Indians, either—
certainly not like the Iroquoians or Algonquians of the
Northeast. Pueblo people tended to be brown-skinned,
with rather broad, flat noses and large mouths. Pueblo
women were frequently plump.

Farming, of course, had been the Pueblo occupation
for centuries, and considering the results they achieved
in such dry country, they must be counted among the
world's finest farmers. Unlike the Hohokam, they depended more on underground moisture than on irrigation. Pueblo fields often lay miles from the pueblo itself,
over the beds of underground streams. Each morning
the tireless Pueblo men would trek to the fields, sometimes a distance of ten or twenty miles. Horseless, they
did their own plowing, breaking up the ground with a
digging stick about five feet long. Old men took care of
the weeding, old women and children were put to work
scaring off crows. The Pueblo wives remained behind,
busy with their pottery and weaving.

The houses belonged to the women and remained
with them all their lives. Since there was little warfare, there was never a shortage of men, and so each
Pueblo man took only a single wife, and lived at her
house. As in all matrilineal cultures, the uncle, not the

father, played the key role in raising children. A man's family responsibilities lay at the house of his mother and sisters, and he was little more than a friend to his own children.

The life of a young Pueblo Indian was a constant round of ceremony. It began on a child's twentieth day of life, when he had to be formally presented to the sun and given a name. Later, at about the age of eight, Pueblo boys were introduced to the rain spirits, and still later were initiated into one of the Pueblo's religious societies.

Pueblo religion was the most complicated ever evolved by American Indians. There were festivals galore, some held every year, some every two years, some even less frequently. The rising of each moon called forth special rituals. The many religious societies had distinctive costumes and masks, and each had its special role to play in the intricate mosaic of Pueblo religious life.

The object of all Pueblo prayer, of course, was to bring rain. There were many supernatural beings who had to be propitiated, beginning with Mother Earth and Father Sky. Those who got the most attention were the rain-gods, known by the Hopi word, *"kachinas."* The kachinas were friendly gods who interceded on man's behalf with the Spider Woman, the sun's wife, who spun the rain clouds. From July until January each year men wearing the gaudy masks of the different kachinas danced in the plazas, begging for rain. The festivals were enlivened by the *koshare,* a society of

clowns painted all over in black-and-white stripes, and
other clowns known as the *goyemshi*, "Mudheads," who
represented the first men who lived on earth. An important part of Pueblo religion was the prayer stick, a
gaily painted, feather-decked wand that was left in
cornfields and at springs, as an offering to the spirits
of those places.

The center of Pueblo religious activity was the kiva.
Only men could enter a kiva, and in some pueblos,
especially among the Zuni, the initiated men would go
into retreat for weeks at a time, organizing the festivals
and communing with the spirits. The kiva had a
wooden roof and sides of mud or stone; there was
always a square hole in the floor, to symbolize the hole

through which the first men were supposed to have come up out of the earth long ago.

The Snake Ceremony was only one of many that centered around the kiva. In this ritual, snakes were gathered from far and wide—the four winds—and were brought to the kiva, where for nine days they were washed, purified, and prayed over. The men of the religious society remained cooped up with the snakes all during this time, finally emerging into the plaza with the snakes held in their mouths. They would dance all day, holding the snakes, to bring rain, and then the reptiles would be taken back to the desert and released, messengers from the people to the gods of rain.

The Hopi and the Zuni are the two best known of the Pueblo tribes, but there are others, such as the Keres, Towa, and Tiwa Indians. They live in eastern New Mexico, along the rivers, and their culture shows the influence of the Indians of the Plains. These pueblo dwellers were more warlike, less placid. They did not

Hopi prayer stick

Hopi pottery jug

have the same elaborate religious organizations. There was more emphasis on individual achievement and less on community activity. Today, the important government atomic research center of Los Alamos employs many of these Eastern, or River Pueblo people, and they have adapted almost completely to the white man's world. In the farming villages of the Hopi and Zuni, change has been slower, but it is coming. Pueblo women still make their superb pottery, but mostly because white tourists like to buy it. The old men gather in the kivas, but their sons and grandsons show less interest in the complex religion of yesterday. The festivals that are still held are often put on for the benefit of tourists. Right now, Hopi and Zuni pueblos are like living museums, and Pueblo ways are followed not so much for their own sake as to satisfy the white visitors. A civilization that stretches back thousands of years, in almost unbroken sequence to Cochise days, is gradually being absorbed into the bustling white world around it.

PIMA AND PAPAGO, HOPI AND ZUNI, all were peaceful growers of corn. Though the differences between the tribes were considerable, they all shared a common outlook on life, and all spoke languages of the Uto-Aztecan family, common throughout Mexico and the American Southwest.

Outsiders came among them, beginning perhaps about A.D. 1200, filtering down in little nomadic bands out of the North. They came out of Canada, speaking singsong Athabascan dialects. Knowing nothing of agri-

culture, they were hunters, killers. They brought with them the sturdy sinew-backed bow, against which the bent sticks of the Pueblo people were no match. Unwanted, feared, they forced their way into the farm country. The pueblo dwellers called them *apachu,* meaning "stranger," "enemy." One band of *apachu,* choosing north-central New Mexico as its raiding ground, came to be known as *apachu nabahu,* "enemies of the cultivated fields." Eventually these Indians were called Navaho, and their related fellow nomads Apache.

They stared at the impressive apartment houses of the village people, and raided and harried them, but did not copy them. The Navaho, as they began to settle down in the Southwest, lived in a lodge called a *hogan,* built from a tripod frame of logs covered with earth. They did a little farming, but never could match the Pueblo Indians' patient way with corn and beans.

Instead, the Navaho, unable to hunt in the desert, went in for raising livestock. They kept sheep, and later, when the Spanish brought them, horses. Taking a casual approach toward other people's property, the Navaho specialized in stealing livestock from the villagers.

They borrowed the idea of the loom from the Pueblos, and their earliest blankets were in Pueblo style. Surprisingly, the former nomads took well to weaving and quickly outstripped their tutors. Navaho blankets soon became the best in the Southwest, and an important trade item. To this day, blanket weaving is one of the chief Navaho industries, and many an Easterner —myself included—proudly decorates his home with a product of a Navaho loom.

The Navaho also borrowed some religious ideas from the pueblo dwellers, though they never attained any real depth or complexity of ritual. They had masked dancers at their festivals, in imitation of Hopi and Zuni, and they had the beginnings of a mother-clan system also. When a man married, he built a hogan next to that of his wife's parents. He never spoke to his mother-in-law, for fear of going insane if he did. The Navaho also had a great fear of death and the evil spirits that death brought; when a Navaho died in a house, that house had to be destroyed. To avoid this, old or dying Navaho were very often moved out of the hogan into a temporary shelter. Burial was accompanied by purification ceremonies for the mourners.

While the Navaho settled down and took up sheep raising, their cousins, the Apache, stayed on the warpath. They remained as they had been in the north woods, primitive, cruel, warlike. The Apache of the eastern range of their territory had no clan system, no agriculture, no weaving, no real religion. They lived off their neighbors, looting and pillaging. The Western Apache, though, were less fierce; while still basically a plundering breed, they developed crude agriculture in imitation of their neighbors the Pima (but among the Apache it was the women who did the farming) and also went in for basketwork, like the Basketmakers of fifteen centuries before them. These western Apaches, who lived in *wickiups*, domed brush huts, borrowed the Navaho clan systems and religious beliefs.

The peace-loving farming Indians of the Southwest posed no problems for the white men who came to settle there. The Apache and Navaho did. Fierce, unpredictable, these Indians would swoop down to steal horses from the white men and to harass them in many ways. The patient pueblo dwellers might sigh and accept the wild ones as just part of life, but the white men fought back. Navaho country became part of the United States in 1848, and for twenty years American troops struggled to subdue the troublesome Indians. The job was finally done by the scout Kit Carson during the Civil War. Instead of chasing the Navaho into the canyons, where they could dig in and defend themselves forever, Carson took a different tack. He killed their sheep and burned their corn, starving them into submission. For four years, the Navaho were kept imprisoned in military camps until, in 1868, they were

released on a promise never to fight again, a promise that they have kept.

The even wilder Apache also had to be subdued. Some tribes of Apache surrendered quickly and settled down on reservations to become farmers and cattlemen. Others, especially the Eastern Apache, resisted stubbornly, under such warrior-chiefs as Cochise and Geronimo. After long and bloody conflict they, too, were rounded up, transferred first to Florida, then to Alabama, and finally to Oklahoma, where some of them settled. The rest were eventually allowed to return to New Mexico, tamed and ready to become law-abiding farmers.

No part of North America has had a longer history of human occupation than the Southwest. Once Folsom Man speared bison there, and before him even more shadowy hunters ranged the long-gone forests. Then came the Cochise people, grinders of seeds, and their successors, the agricultural Hohokam and Mogollon, and the Anasazi, builders of apartment houses, tireless tillers of the fields. Last arrived the intruders from the North, Apache and Navaho. The story of the American Southwest is an epic of man's struggle against the desert, and a hundred centuries or more of continuous human occupation tell how successful that struggle has been.

THE LAND OF
MANY LANGUAGES

BEYOND THE DESERTS OF ARIZONA LIES FERTILE, GREEN California, today the most populous state of the Union, famous for its sunshine, its motion pictures, and its smog. California once was Indian country, long before anyone had dreamed of automobiles or cameras. No part of North America was closer to paradise.

Paradise? Of course. The weather was mild. Winter never came to California. The trees were forever green, and one had only to shake them, and down would come acorns and other seeds good to eat. Warfare was unknown, for why fight when everyone has all that he needs? No one had to wear clothing, or to build shelters against the cold. The living was easy. *Too* easy, in fact, for much of a civilization to develop. California, hundreds of years ago, was a Garden of Eden where man lived a relaxed, blissful life.

California in Indian days brings to mind another Biblical parallel, that of the Tower of Babel. For this was a land of many languages. Nowhere else in the

world were so many tongues spoken in so small a geographical area. There were more than one hundred fifty
languages in California, and every one of the major Indian language families was represented, even such
Eastern ones as Algonquian and Muskhogean. California was inhabited by hundreds of small tribes, each
one remaining in a fixed spot, each speaking its own
dialect.

How did such a bewildering linguistic situation oc-
cur? Did Indians migrate to California from all over
North America, as white men have been doing for the
past hundred years? Was there a flow of Iroquoian and
Athabascan and Algonquian and Muskhogean settlers
trekking across the plains?

Quite the contrary. The migration seems to have
been in the other direction. As anthropologists recon-
struct it, there were successive waves of emigrants
coming out of Asia over a period of thousands of years.
Each particular group spoke its own kind of language.
Each group crossed from Siberia into Alaska, and pro-
gressed down the western coast of North America until
it reached California.

Some members of each wandering group must have
been satisfied enough with the California climate to
decide to settle down right there. The others kept on
going, heading to their ultimate destinations in New
England, Georgia, Ohio, or Mexico. Gradually, as the
centuries passed, little pockets of Indian tribes accumulated in California, left behind by the waves of immigrants as they passed by.

The living was easy there. The chief food was acorns, which were gathered and stored in the shell until needed. It was the simplest thing in the world to "harvest" acorns, which dropped from the trees by the thousands. But making them edible was a different matter, calling for some ingenuity. Acorns contain tannic acid, which makes them bitter to the taste. After who knows how many hundreds of years, some unknown genius discovered that acorns could be used for food if pounded into meal and soaked in water until the bitter taste was gone. Then a kind of bread could be made of the acorn meal.

This was the staff of life in Indian California. There were other edible seeds, too, and the Indians filled out their diet by fishing and by hunting small game.

Only one group of California Indians were farmers —the Yuma, who lived along the Colorado River. They learned something about agriculture from the Pima to the east, and planted corn, squash, and other familiar Indian crops. No Indian farmers ever had it easier than the Yuma. There was no need for them to beg for rain, to fertilize their fields, or to hold lengthy planting and harvest festivals. All they had to do was scatter the seed, and the rich soil and the beneficent climate took care of the rest.

This left the Yuma free for religious observances of another kind, those dealing with war and with death. They were not warlike in the Apache sense, but rather in the way of the Indians of the East, fighting as a way of winning spiritual power. In this they were unlike most of the other Indians of California, who did not fight at all.

The Yuma were typical California Indians in their attitude toward death. They were all obsessed by it. Why, in this mild and sunny land, the Indians should have fastened so much interest on the end of life is anyone's guess. California Indian death customs cast a dark shadow over the Eden of the Pacific.

The Yuma burned their dead. They built great pyres of logs, high as a house, placing the dead person upon it clad in fine clothes (though in life they usually went almost naked). The entire clan gathered and danced all night, throwing gifts on the blazing pyre, and afterward the house of the dead man was burned —no great loss among the Yumas, who, like most California Indians, lived in flimsy huts of brush or logs. Several times a year thereafter, relatives of the dead would come together to hold a mourning ceremony. But it was forbidden to speak of the dead in any way; to call a man an orphan was the deadliest insult the Yuma knew.

The tribes farther west did not bother with agriculture at all, and lived the simplest possible existence, gathering nuts and seeds, wearing few clothes, and devoting much of their time to matters of religion and tribal organization. Clans mostly followed the pattern of father-descent, and nearly all tribes were divided into moieties as well. An Indian married into the op-

posite moiety, but usually without any special ceremony. The major ceremonies were reserved for death.

It was dangerous to bury one's own dead, or to
handle the cremation, where that was the practice. The
relatives of the dead man would send for members of
the opposite moiety to take care of the funeral arrangements. The tribes close to the shore used shell
"money" made of clamshells strung on cord and, curi-
ously, the men of the other moiety paid the mourners
for the privilege of burying their dead. (Later, the
shell payments were usually returned after the dead
one was safely in the spirit world.) The dead person's
house and possessions were burned with him, his name
was never mentioned again, and an involved series of
rituals was adopted to prevent the spirit from returning
to the village. On the anniversary of the death, festivals
of mourning were held, relatives of the dead person
gave gifts to the rest of the tribe, and long chants of
grief were sung.

There were also ceremonies to mark the coming of
age. Girls, when they reached eleven or twelve, would
fast and be subjected to speeches from the elders of
the tribe, who would explain the importance of mother-
hood and hard work (hard work by Californian standards, that is; any other Indian would have considered
such a life a perpetual vacation).

Boys had to go through a more complicated proce-
dure. They were supposed to have visions as they
entered manhood, but whereas in other Indian tribes
the visions were brought about by fasting and praying,

the Californians used a drug. It was made from the pounded root of the datura, or Jimson weed. Old men of the tribe would carefully administer the drug, which caused hallucinations. If a boy had a particularly powerful "visit from the spirit world" while under the influence of the drug, he might become a shaman when he grew older. A few tribes had more taxing ordeals. The Luiseño, for instance, sent boys out to lie naked on anthills before they could enter manhood.

Southern California was the home of many tribes which are generally grouped together under the name of Mission Indians, because of the Spanish missions that brought Christianity to them in the latter part of the eighteenth century. North of Mission Indian country, in the Sacramento Valley, lived five tribes whose language, Penutian, was found nowhere else, along with a highly diversified assemblage of Indian tribes speaking Algonquian, Siouan, and Athabascan tongues. There, basket-weaving became a high art. Among one tribe, the Pomo, the stitches were so fine that a microscope is needed to count them. The brilliant plumage of California's many birds went to ornament these baskets in a spectacularly colorful way. When Sir Francis Drake visited California in 1578, he met a group of Pomo who showed him their baskets, "so well wrought as to hold water."

Along the coast, in northern California, some of the Indian tribes took to the sea, a rarity among Indians. The Chumash, a large tribe that once lived along the coast near Santa Barbara, built unusual canoes out of pine planks lashed with animal sinew, made watertight with asphalt.

A hundred different religions flourished in the California of the Indians. Most of them centered around the death obsession, but the details varied from tribe to tribe. The Patwin, Pomo, and Maidu held yearly dances called "Kuksu," in which the dancers wore crowns of feathers, but their neighbors had entirely different rites and dances. It is not easy to talk about the customs of the California Indians as a group.

Except for the Yuma of western California, the Californian Indians were not, as we have noted, fighters. When quarrels sprang up between tribes, the differences were usually settled by payments of shell money, or by a combat between two appointed tribal champions, not by war. There was no prestige attached to being a warrior, no compulsion to collect scalps or count coup.

This very peacefulness did California's Indians in

when the white man finally came to stay, late in the eighteenth century. The first settlers were Spanish, and they brought priests who took charge of the Indians. A string of missions was established along seven hundred miles of the coast, and the Indians were taken from their peaceful seed-gathering life, converted to Christianity en masse, and turned into farmers who were little more than slaves. One Spanish priest, referring to his Indian charges as "lazy, stupid, gluttonous, timorous," declared, "I have never seen any of them laugh, I have never seen a single one look anyone in the face. They have the air of taking no interest in anything."

The death rate among the Mission Indians was dreadfully high. Those who rebelled against the rule of the *padres* were imprisoned, flogged, or shackled. Even so, the Indians by and large thrived during the Mission era. Peacefully, placidly, they allowed themselves to be turned into farm hands. But the priests left when California passed from the rule of Spain to that of the Republic of Mexico, and soon after to that of the United States. The missions were broken up. The Indians, who had become totally dependent on the guidance they received from the Spanish priests, were cast adrift, left to shift for themselves.

Then, in 1848, gold was discovered in California. Hordes of white men streamed into the territory, seeking their fortunes. They were a rough-and-ready bunch who would not coddle the Indians as the Spanish had, and decided to exterminate them instead. Before the gold rush, there had been at least one hundred thousand Indians in California. By 1859, only thirty thousand were left. Between 1850 and 1859, the United States Government paid the State of California $924,-259 to reimburse it for the expenses of the campaign against the Indians. Indian land was confiscated. One government official, in 1858, talked about the "great cause of civilization, which, in the natural course of things, must exterminate Indians."

Some of them survived, particularly in southern California, beyond the gold-mining region. They were given scraps of land as their reservations. Many tribes died out of sheer sorrow, but a few held on, and today there are still some ten thousand Indians in California on the reservations. Ironically, a few of them have become millionaires. They happened to own the land on which the flamboyant resort town of Palm Springs was built, and they were able to make their rights stand up in court.

WEST OF THE ROCKIES, east of the Sierras and Cascades, lies a great stretch of barren land. The northern part of this region is high and dry and barren, and is known as the Plateau. The southern part is low and dry and barren, and is known as the Great Basin. Neither the Plateau nor the Great Basin gets much rain, and there are few rivers, few lakes. Today, thanks to modern irrigation and to the birth of the mining industry, this area—Nevada, Utah, Idaho, and parts of the surrounding states—is thriving and expanding. But before the days of the white man, the Basin and the Plateau contained the poorest, simplest Indians of North America.

There were many tribes, but not many Indians. In that harsh country, it was impossible to be fruitful and multiply. The little seminomadic bands lived in small family groups, widely scattered, constantly on the move. The struggle for food absorbed all the energies of such Indians as the Ute, the Paiute, the Havasupai, and the others.

Once the Great Basin had had hundreds of lakes, ranging upward in size to mighty Lake Bonneville, whose shrunken remnant we call Great Salt Lake today. Those lakes dried up ten thousand years ago. The parched ground is anything but hospitable to vegetation. Mountains at east and west block the rain. The desperately poor Indians who lived in the Basin were contemptuously called "Digger Indians" by the whites who saw them grubbing for roots. There was no agriculture, and hardly any hunting or fishing, not in a land where the wild life consisted largely of grasshoppers, rats, and lizards. (The Indians ate all three.)

Food was the overriding need. The Basin Indians spun nets of hemp thirty feet long to catch jack rabbits. They rode herd on grasshoppers, driving them into trenches and roasting them alive, then grinding them into flour. When they were very lucky, they encountered herds of pronghorn antelope, and stalked them tensely, driving them with torches into brush corrals to be slaughtered. Snakes, gophers, squirrels, brush fowl, sage hens all formed part of the diet. In the less bleak parts of the Basin there were acorns to be gathered, and the seeds of the piñon pine, a white man's delicacy today.

The rugged climate, too, posed problems. The summers were fiercely hot. Death Valley, in the Basin, is one of the hottest places on earth; the temperatures sometimes reach 140° in summer. For half the year, with the swollen sun glaring down, the Basin Indians wore little or nothing, and spent their days searching for shade. But then came the winters, as cold as the summers were hot. Animal life fled; food was unobtainable; the poverty-stricken, hungry Basin Indians huddled together for warmth, sometimes turning to cannibalism in their hunger. They covered themselves with robes of rabbitskin, or perhaps with a tattered buffalo hide obtained somehow from one of the Plains tribes on the other side of the Rockies. Their dwellings were domed wickiups of poles and brush, built over pits in the manner of the Basketmakers of centuries before.

Where life is a constant struggle for the basic things of existence, there is no time for development of elaborate customs. The Basin Indians had no clan system, no marriage taboos. Young people married any available neighbor, and roamed nomadically with husband's parents or bride's, as they wished. Since the tribes were so small, it often happened that a man had to take two wives, or, what is more unusual among Indians, that a woman married two husbands.

There was little in the way of religion, either: no organized festivals and rituals, only a superstition-ridden fear of the spirit world. Most of the tribes had witch doctors or shamans, but their role was a simple one. They healed the sick, or tried to, by incantation and prayer. If a patient died after treatment, the shaman might find himself accused of witchcraft. The sick who did not respond to treatment got short shrift; in a poverty-stricken society, there is no room for those who cannot provide for themselves, and the aged, sick, and infirm were left to die when the tribe moved on. Newborn infants might also be abandoned to spare them the endless round of hardships that life in the Basin meant.

There was no war in the Great Basin, for the Basin Indians possessed nothing anyone else might want. Their arts were confined to weaving and basketwork. They had little mythology, few traditions. When the white man came, these insignificant "Digger Indians" were trampled underfoot, ignored or despised. Most of them finally abandoned the nomadic, food-gathering life, and became laborers in the white man's mining camps, or else simply beggars. They still live that shadowy life, excluded from the booming growth taking place in their old territories.

The Plateau Indians to the north lived something of the same life as the Basin folk, only it was not quite as harsh. In the higher land, rain came more frequently, food was easier to obtain. There were some twenty-five tribes in the Plateau area, of four different language groups. The most common language family was Shoshonean, a member of the Uto-Aztecan group and therefore distantly related to the language spoken in the pueblos. (Most of the Basin tribes also spoke Shoshonean dialects.)

Two mighty rivers slice through the barren uplands of the Plateau: the Columbia and the Snake. Both abound with salmon, so the tribes living in the northwestern part of the Plateau were fishermen, and whole villages turned out in spring to trap or spear the thronging fish as they struggled upstream. While some Plateau tribes had to rely on seeds and roots, others became passable hunters. Tribes of the eastern Plateau, like the Shoshone and Nez Perce, obtained horses, and lived after the fashion of the Plains Indians, hunting the buffalo that roamed as far west as Montana. At the opposite end of the Plateau, a few tribes like the Kutenai built bark canoes and skin-covered coracles, and became expert rivermen.

So far as tribal organization went, the Plateau tribes were as simple as their cousins in the Great Basin. They had no confederacies or nations, no clans, no moieties. The "tribes" were little more than loosely held together bands of people speaking the same language. Even the tribal leadership was a hit-or-miss business; some tribes had no chiefs at all, others selected them to serve for only a short time.

Like many Indian groups who have no very strong characteristics of their own, the Plateau people were easily influenced by their neighbors. In the east, they came under the sway of the hard-riding warriors of the Plains, and took over some ideas about prestige and valor that were otherwise alien to their own way of life. From the west, they were influenced by the property-conscious, seagoing Indians of the Pacific Coast, whom we shall meet in the next chapter.

The rituals of Plateau life dealt largely with matters of food: how to obtain it, how to prepare it, how to divide it. They had medicine men and beliefs in the spirit world, but were too busy hunting and gathering food to develop any very complex religious patterns.

They were among the last Indians to encounter white men. The Lewis and Clark expedition of 1804–1806 passed through the Plateau country, and we are all familiar with the story of Sacajawea, the Shoshone woman who served as that party's guide and interpreter. There was no real friction between the whites and the Plateau people for many years, since the settlers who came did not stop in the bleak inland Plateau, but passed on through to the Pacific Coast. Only later, when railroads were built through the Plateau Indians' territory, was there fighting, and from 1852 to 1880 a series of little wars and revolts brought bloodshed to the land, ending, of course, in the subjugation of the Indians, the breaking up of the old way of life, and their confinement to reservations.

Not all Indians had complex societies, as we have seen in this chapter. Some, like those of California, found life so easy that they had no spur to progress. Others, the Basin Indians and those of the Plateau, suffered from the opposite drawback. The endless struggle simply to survive sapped all the vigor from them, and they lived in poverty and simplicity until the time came for them to pass from the scene.

13

POTLATCHES AND
TOTEM POLES

A CHAIN OF ROBUST MOUNTAINS RUNS PARALLEL TO the Pacific Coast, not very far inland. From Puget Sound to Alaska, those mountains come down almost to the water's edge, leaving only a narrow strip of coastal land.

So far as climate goes, that coastal strip is lucky. The Japan Current comes up out of Asia, carrying warm water across to the Aleutians and down the coast, bringing a mild warmth to the Far North. Moisture-laden breezes blow in from the ocean and, meeting the impassable wall of the mountains, drop their burden as life-giving rain. Fast-flowing rivers, slashing through the peaks, bring fresh water to the coastal strip, and those rivers throng with salmon and other fish, swimming up from the Pacific each year in such numbers that, as goggle-eyed white explorers reported, "you could walk across on their backs."

It is an unusual part of the continent, that coastal strip, and in Indian days it harbored one of the most

intricate and fascinating of all the Indian cultures. The
wealthy, densely populated towns of the Pacific Northwest achieved heights of civilization matched nowhere
else in North America except in the Pueblo and the
Temple Mound society.

The Indians of the region were rich in nature's
bounty. It was not the pick-up-seeds kind of bounty
found in California; more effort was needed, but the
rewards were correspondingly great. Unlike all the
other important Indian civilizations, that of the Pacific
Northwest Indians did not depend on agriculture. They
raised a little tobacco, it is true, but the prime activity
was fishing. The sea yielded prodigious harvests. Salmon
in the rivers, cod and halibut just off shore, sea lion
and sea otter farther out, and, in the deep waters, great
whales, all contributed to the wealth of the coast peoples. Sea life spawned there as it does in few other
parts of the world.

The mild, wet climate was ideal for forest growth.
Splendid stands of Douglas fir to the north, towering
redwoods farther south, and pine everywhere afforded
an inexhaustible supply of wood: wood for houses,
wood for canoes, wood for masks and furniture and
utensils, wood for the totem poles that ornamented
every village. Before the white man came, the coast
peoples had no metal for axes or saws, but they managed
to fell the big trees, to split them into boards, to trim
and shape them, to join them without nails.

Wealthy and self-confident, bold and high-spirited,
they developed a civilization and an art that bear the

stamp of their adventurous souls. Their gaudy, colorful way of life revolved around personal prestige, the possession of property, the attainment of glory. In this, they may seem to share the ideals of the Plains Indians. It should soon become apparent, however, that the coast people were as different from the freewheeling horsemen of the Plains as they were from the stolid, placid farmers of the pueblos.

The lower part of the coastal strip, beginning in northern California, and continuing up to about where the Canadian border now lies, was inhabited by Indians who did not really share in the highly developed life of their relatives to the north. These Indians of Oregon and Washington were not poor by Plateau or Basin standards, but they were far from attaining the wealth of the North. They lived on rivers and bays rather than on the coast itself, and spoke dialects of the Plateau language known as "Salish." Their art and life was simple, reminding us more of the Plateau cultures than anything else. They seem to be Plateau Indians, living in a land of somewhat greater opportunity.

Perhaps, seven or eight hundred years ago, all the Indians of the Pacific Coast lived in similar simplicity. In fairly recent times, probably only from 1500 on, there was a great flowering of civilization in the North, chiefly on the coastal islands of Alaska and British Columbia. The Tlingit, the Haida, the Nootka, and others took up their lives as whalers, sea-raiders, and builders of totem poles.

Physically, these seagoing Indians were quite different from the ones already discussed. They tended to be light-skinned, short and stocky, with deep chests and powerful shoulders. Their hair sometimes had a coppery red tinge, in contrast to the almost universal black hair elsewhere. Most unusually, these were hairy Indians. Many of the men wore mustaches and even beards. All other Indians of North and South America had sparse and scanty beards, and always remained clean-shaven, so these bewhiskered Indians of the Pacific Northwest are unique on that count.

They lived in towns built along the island shore or, if they dwelt on the mainland, on the banks and mouths of rivers. Their houses were massive plank buildings, which among the Haida were as much as one hundred twenty feet long, forty feet wide, and housed up to three dozen people. The rectangular wooden houses, made of big beams supported by heavy corner posts, looked something like the large unpainted barns of old New England. White explorers coming upon such dwellings on Puget Sound found it hard to believe that they were built without saws or axes and that their construction used not a single nail. By dint of skillful squaring and joining, the Indians were able to fit their planks together so well that no nails were necessary.

Some tribes, such as the Kwakiutl and the Nootka, were not inclined to live in one place too long. They liked to move periodically from one fishing ground to another, and one tribe might shuttle among three or four different village sites. They kept permanent house frames set up at each site, and would dismantle the

walls of their houses and take them along when they
moved.

Inside these big houses, life resembled that within an
Iroquois longhouse. Each family had its own raised
cubicle along the wall, and a row of fires blazed down
the middle of the earthen floor. The walls were often
made of movable slats that could be lifted when smoke
got too thick within the windowless house. When
someone died in a house, the body would be carried
out through an opening between the wall slats, rather
than through the main door, in hopes of fooling the
spirit and preventing it from finding its way back into
the house.

This fear of the dead is an Indian attitude we have
seen before. As did other tribes, the Northwesterners
went to great extents to keep people from dying in their
houses, often taking them outside as their last moments
approached. A house in which someone had died frequently had to be taken down. Touching a dead body
was dangerous, and those who performed funeral rites
had to undergo purification afterward. The name of a
dead man could not be uttered for a year or more after
his burial. Even when his name was the name of some
common animal or tree, it had to be avoided. If, for
instance, a man named Black Bear died, the community
would, for a while, have to refer to black bears as
"creatures the color of night who walk on their hind
legs."

Religion, among these sea peoples, was a hectic and
strenuous matter. As Ruth Benedict puts it in her

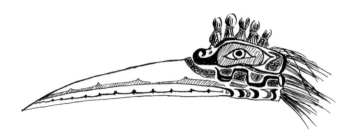

famous anthropological study, *Patterns of Culture:* "In their religious ceremonies the final thing they strove for was ecstasy. The chief dancer, at least at the high point of his performance, should lose normal control of himself and be rapt into another state of existence. He should froth at the mouth, tremble violently and abnormally, do deeds which would be terrible in a normal state. Some dancers were tethered by four ropes held by attendants, so that they might not do irreparable damage in their frenzy."

The Northwestern Indians saw themselves surrounded by a multitude of animal spirits, most of them unfriendly. It was the job of the shaman to placate these hostile spirits and to praise the friendly ones. Only in that way could the salmon, the otter, and the whale, on which the community's wealth depended, be persuaded to return to the hunting grounds the following season. Costumed in elaborate masks, dancing with incredible energy, the shamans performed their strenuous rites with a vigor and gusto that seem astonishing to us. They might dance for days at a time, sinister and terrible in their bearskin robes and their weird hook-nosed masks of red and yellow and green. Sometimes they danced with glowing coals in their hands, playing with them, hurling them insanely at the assembled villagers, even putting them in their mouths. And as they danced, they sang about such fierce spirits as this one:

> How shall we hide from the bear that is moving
>   all around the world?
> Let us crawl underground! Let us cover our backs
>   with dirt that the terrible great bear from
>   the north of the world may not find us.

And they would chant the praises of horrifying creatures:

> Great is the fury of this great supernatural one.
> He will carry men in his arms and torment them.
> He will devour them skin and bones, crushing flesh
>   and bone with his teeth.

It was a society in which dark terrors did not lie very far beneath the surface of existence. But the Northwesterners were businesslike and brisk in their pursuit of wealth, however barbaric their religious practices may seem to us. They had capitalists and poor men, and those who were rich were very rich indeed.

Wealth was measured in terms of property—slaves, blankets, food stores, wives, houses, boats. Slave-raiding was a frequent pastime, and in the richest villages slaves made up nearly a third of the population. One wealthy chief of the early nineteenth century was said to have "nearly fifty male and female slaves," according to a white man taken captive by his tribe.

Wealth was inherited, and the wealthiest families

had the highest social standing. There was a sort of Indian aristocracy of wealth, a "social register." A man not born into the wealthy families could improve his lot by hard work and cleverness, so that members of the "lower middle class" could work their way up the ladder. Only the slaves had no rights; captives from other tribes, they were regarded as property, could not own anything themselves, and frequently were sacrificed to mark an important man's death or to bring a blessing upon a newly constructed house.

The richest man in each town was the chief. He owned the town's hunting and fishing grounds and the whaling or war canoes by which the town got its livelihood. Descent was through the father's line, and the chief was usually the eldest son of the previous chief. If a man lost his wealth through incompetence or accident, he would lose his power in the community as well, though he would keep his titles of nobility. Just as today there are some nearly penniless dukes and counts in Europe, descendants of the once-wealthy, so, too, were there among the Indians of the Northwest pathetic noblemen who had the proper ancestry, but had lost the power that went with their rank.

In our society, a person proves his wealth by spending money. He buys expensive motor cars, big houses, fine jewelry. He travels to other countries. He eats at costly restaurants. Above all, he makes sure that he is *seen.* This is what the economist Thorstein Veblen called "conspicuous consumption." Many a man, trying too hard to impress others this way, has spent himself right into bankruptcy.

The Indian way to demonstrate wealth was to give it away. We saw this among the Plains Indians, with their Give Away Feasts. But on the Pacific coast the giving away of wealth became a way of life—one of the strangest aspects of this very unusual culture.

Small gifts were an everyday part of Northwestern life, just as tipping is for us. Among the Tlingit or the Haida, a man might give away a blanket or two whenever he was invited to a feast, when he joined in a religious dance, or even when his name was mentioned in tribal councils. On certain major occasions, though, a great feast called a "potlatch" was given, in which the process reached its ultimate flowering.

The word "potlatch" comes from a Chinook Indian word, *patshatl,* meaning "giving." A man might give a potlatch to celebrate a birth in his family, a death, a marriage, or his own inheritance of a chieftainship. A chief might buy one of the members of his tribe back from slavery in another tribe through a potlatch. If an important chief had suffered a humiliation, he could re-establish his prestige through a potlatch. A leading figure in a Northwestern town might give three or four grand potlatches during his lifetime, and a number of lesser ones.

A grand potlatch required years of planning. The guests had to be chosen with care, since the purpose of the potlatch was to impress, and one had to invite rich men to such an affair. Worldly goods had to be accumulated. Specific gifts had to be set aside for particular guests.

A potlatch was a kind of contest, a war fought not with weapons but with property. Guests would arrive in their canoes on the great day, and would be taken to the house of the potlatch-giver, where the feasting would continue for several days. Of course, the guests had to be handsomely fed. When everyone had gorged himself to the full, the main business of the potlatch would begin.

The host would start by praising himself in terms of the most shameless self-advertising. Ruth Benedict, in her study of the Kwakiutl Indians of Vancouver Is-

Two Northwest Indian shamans dressed as Raven and Wolf greeting each other on arrival for a potlatch

land, gives us a few examples of these "hymns of self-glorification":

> I am the first of the tribes,
> I am the only one of the tribes.
> The chiefs of the tribes are only local chiefs.
> I am the only one among the tribes.
> I search among all the invited chiefs for greatness
>   like mine.
> I cannot find one chief among the guests.
>
> I am he who gives these sea otters to the chiefs the
>   guests, the chiefs of the tribes.
> I am he who gives canoes to the chiefs the guests,
>   the chiefs of the tribes.
>
> I am the great chief who vanquishes. . . .
> I sneer at the chiefs under the true great chief,
> I am the great chief who makes people ashamed.

This boasting now had to be followed up by proof. The potlatch-giver had to shame his rivals in fact as well as by words. There were two ways of doing this: by giving away more property than the rivals could afford to return with interest, and by destroying property to show one's indifference to it. Destruction of goods was considered the best way to win prestige.

At a potlatch, the guests would sit round a fire on which fish oil was constantly thrown as a sign of the potlatch-giver's wealth. The more oil thrown, the higher the fire blazed, which made things uncomfortable for the guests sitting round it; but, for the sake of their own pride, they had to remain seated in their places no matter how hot the fire became, or else they

Thin copper medal, sign of wealth

would admit defeat. The host might commence by sending for canoes and having them broken up and hurled on the fire. He might order a valued slave forward, club him with the special ornamented club known as a "slave killer," and scornfully toss his scalp to his particular rival. Most impressive of all was the destruction of a "copper."

These coppers were tokens of wealth—thin sheets of the metal as much as three feet long, etched with ornamental designs. Each copper had its own name and ancestry; its value was not in its metal, but in the arbitrary worth the Indians assigned to it. A copper that had belonged to many great chiefs might change hands for ten thousand blankets or more.

At a potlatch, a famous copper might be given away, or it might be destroyed—an act very much like that of lighting a cigar with a thousand-dollar bill. Ruth Benedict tells us that a chief destroying a copper might make a speech of this sort:

"Furthermore such is my pride, that I will kill on this fire my copper Dandalayu which is groaning in my house. You all know how much I paid for it. I bought it for four thousand blankets. Now I will break it in order to vanquish my rival. I will make my house a fighting place for you, my tribe. Be happy, chiefs, this is the first time that so great a potlatch has been given."

Complete destruction of the copper was not necessary. The chief might simply cut out one section of it and throw it on the fire, making it necessary for his rival to mutilate an equally valuable copper in the same way.

After destroying a copper and killing a slave or two, the potlatch-giver would proceed to load his guests down with gifts, calling each guest up in the order of his rank and giving him something worthy of his wealth. The host would insult his guests, telling them, "I give you this mountain of blankets (or canoes, or slaves, or whatever) to show my greatness. But you cannot equal my gift. You say you are rich, but you are not my equal in any way."

These insults could be met by counter-insults. If a guest thought his gift was too small, he might drag it along the ground to show his contempt. This was bold and risky, because he would then be called on to prove his merits at a potlatch of his own. When the host had distributed everything, he would fold up his last blanket and ask his guests, "Who wishes to take it?" It was spoken as a challenge, for the man who took it had to give the next potlatch, and it would not go well for him if he failed to outshine the one just held.

A man could easily bankrupt himself by holding

Host chief at potlatch lecturing dancer who wears half mask to indicate that he is a chagrined rival

such a potlatch, but not for long. The potlatch-givers were careful to dispose of only the outward signs of wealth—coppers, blankets, slaves, canoes. The real sources of wealth—fishing and hunting territories—still remained jealously guarded, and so a powerful chief could replenish his "bank account" quickly enough even after a grand potlatch. Furthermore, the giver of a potlatch would regain possessions at the next pot-latch. Among the Kwakiutl, it was considered a mark of shame not to be able to return a potlatch-giver's presents with 100 per cent interest, that is, a twofold return. Someone unable to meet the harsh competition of the potlatch system might leave the tribe and then take his life in humiliation.

The potlatch system probably reached its peak around the eighteenth century. After that the Indians of the Northwest were in contact with white men, and the old values began to break up. Blankets, canoes, and coppers no longer meant as much as they once did, and it was possible for a young Indian of no particular rank to go off on a white man's whaling expedition and earn enough money to make him a rich man in the tribe. This, naturally, turned the old scheme of value topsy-turvy.

The coming of the white man was important, though, in developing one of the most characteristic products of the Indians of the Northwest. This is the totem pole, which seems to be almost entirely a comparatively recent addition to the Northwestern culture pattern.

The basic idea goes back to a time before the white

man. Among the Haida and some of the other North-western tribes, every house originally had a tall pole in front of its entrance, topped with a carved representation of some animal. There seems to have been no particular religious significance to this pole and its ornament.

Later, in the nineteenth century, the poles took on a new meaning. Now each chief would cause the "totem," or sacred animal of his clan, to be carved on his pole, along with representations of important events in the chief's life. If the chief happened to be a member of the Eagle clan and he had once humiliated a chief of the Wolf clan at a potlatch, his pole might show a heroic-looking eagle biting a cowardly-looking wolf. It was all part of the policy of public boasting so important in Northwestern life.

It was the metal tools of the white man that made possible the carving of the towering, fifty-foot-high totem poles with which we are familiar. Some towns might have dozens of the poles—the Haida village of Skidegate had more than fifty—each testifying to the prestige and power of some important noble. The great era of totem-pole-building was from 1840 to 1880, when a group of skilled craftsmen, using the new tools, made a high art of it. (One pole showed the Czar of Russia; this commemorated the sale of Alaska by Russia to the United States in 1867. Several Tlingit poles of the same era showed Abraham Lincoln, complete with top hat and beard!)

The totem-pole era represented the last blossoming

of the remarkable woodworking skill of these seagoing Indians. All of them were master carpenters, even the Tlingit of the North, who had no good wood of their own and had to import cedar and spruce from other tribes. Using chisels made of elkhorn or nephrite (a kind of jade), the coast peoples felled the mighty trees of the inexhaustible forests, and split them into planks by driving wedges of yew wood into the trunks. Their favorite woodworking tool was the adz, which is something like an axe with its blade set at right angles to the handle. They used adzes of bone to chisel and plane as well as to hollow out canoes. (The adz is a common tool in the islands of Polynesia. Since the Indians of the Northwest share many cultural and bodily traits with the Polynesians, it is considered quite possible that numerous islanders journeyed eastward across the Pacific to settle on the western coast of North America and to intermarry with the Indian population there. This would explain the striking differences between the Indians of the Northwest and those of the rest of the Americas. But it ought to be stressed that this is strictly guesswork as of now.)

The coast peoples made canoes of several shapes and many sizes. The general method of building them was the same in all cases. The trunk of the white cedar was used. This handsome tree provided trunks big enough to make canoes more than sixty feet long and eight feet wide. The trunk would be floated to the working place, where it would be shaped and then hollowed out. This was a painstaking process. The workers would char part of the trunk with torches, remove the charred wood with chisels and mauls, then shape the dugout hollow with finer adzes. From time to time they would drill a hole through the sides of the trunk to measure the thickness. Hollowing out a trunk was delicate work, for white cedar splits easily, and a split in the late stages could ruin the work of weeks.

After the body of the canoe had been hollowed into shape, the opening was filled with water, and hot stones dropped in. As the water boiled, the wood softened, allowing the builders to spread the sides of the canoe and insert four-foot-long thwarts to keep them spread. Finally, the high ends of the typical Haida canoe were added; these were made from separate pieces of wood carefully fitted into place and fastened by pegs and lashings. The men then polished the outside of the canoe with sharkskin "to make it slip easily through the water," and decorated the hulls with the brilliant yellows, blacks, and reds typical of Northwestern artistry. Fast-moving and graceful, these Haida canoes were sturdy and, despite their round bottoms, surprisingly sea-worthy even in rough ocean water.

The Nootka, who were the most active whalers of the Northwest, used a somewhat different style of boat, more streamlined, with lower ends and a flatter bottom. When the Nootka went whaling, a dozen or more canoes, each holding ten men, would go to sea. They were under the command of a chief who owned the canoes and claimed to "own" the whale as well. He had the right to strike the first harpoon.

Nootka whalers spent three months praying and purifying themselves before each hunt. They begged the spirits of great harpooners of the past to come to their aid. When a whale was sighted, the chief's canoe approached it first, coming as close as a yard or two from the whale before the harpoon was cast. Nootka harpoons could not be hurled great distances; they had to be thrust into the whale at close range. A strong three-hundred-foot line of cedar-bark rope lay coiled in the chief's canoe, fastened to his harpoon.

The chief struck first, thrusting at the whale's head to avoid the lash of the powerful tail. As he struck, he would drop into the bottom of the boat, while his crew rowed away from the whale with all their strength to avoid being swamped by the convulsions of the angry beast. A particularly bold—or particularly foolish— chief might actually leap onto the back of the whale, staying with it until it submerged. An honored Nootka name, in fact, was "Stepping on a Whale." Since this was a risky and often fatal operation, a chief who had been badly humiliated in a recent potlatch might some- times resort to it. If he survived, he would have re- couped some of his lost prestige; if he perished, he would at least have died heroically and wiped out the stain of his humiliation.

After the chief had thrust his harpoon, the other boats approached in strict order of their leaders' rank and cast their harpoons, too. Forty or fifty harpoons might be cast, until the whale was tangled in dozens of lines. The whalers would let themselves be towed by the whale until its strength was exhausted—some- times it took three or four days—and finally closed in again, hamstringing it by slashing the tendons of its tail with a spade-shaped lance, and killing it with a spear-thrust to the heart. Then began the strenuous task of towing the dead whale to shore, and the laborious operation of stripping it of meat, oil, bone, and sinew, all of which were used by the Indians.

THE CULTURE OF THE POTLATCH-GIVERS was one of the last Indian cultures to develop. It reached its peak between 1500 and 1800, perhaps, as we have noted, under the influence of emigrants from Polynesia. By the time the white men reached the Pacific Northwest, toward the close of the eighteenth century, they found a highly developed civilization there, a strange mixture of barbarism and sophistication.

The first white man to meet these people was Vitus Bering, who saw them in 1741 while exploring the strait that now bears his name. Russia capitalized on Bering's discovery to establish a fur-trading empire in Alaska, which lasted from 1799 to 1867, despite dogged opposition from the Tlingit whose territory it had been.

The Indians farther down the coast fared better. They were visited by many traders, first Spanish and Russian, later English, still later American, and, led by the commerce-minded Chinook, they did business with all the visitors without allowing themselves to be dominated by any of them. It was a time of grandeur for these Indians, who made use of new tools to improve their way of life, carving bigger and better totem poles, using brass kettles for boiling instead of dropping hot stones into pots, and employing nails in their building for the first time. The clumsy Nootka harpoon gave way to guns, and armed with the new weapons the Indians practically exterminated the fur-bearing seals which had been such an important part of their food supply. The collision with the white world eventually produced overwhelming strains in the Northwestern Indian way of life. They had never been a really stable people anyway, with their ecstatic dances and their bizarre boasting, and the influx of new weapons, new diseases, and new whiskey caused their whole social structure to totter.

In 1867, Alaska passed into American hands. American settlers moved into Washington and Oregon, disrupting the lives of the southernmost coast Indians. Those of Canada withstood change longer. But the pressures of the outside world eventually took their toll. The vigor and individuality went out of the Haida and the Tlingit and the others, and they allowed themselves to be absorbed into the invading culture of the white man. There are no more potlatches, no more whale hunts. The coppers and the totem poles now are museum pieces. Shadows and echoes out of the past are all that remain, for the descendants of the potlatch people live like white men, no longer boasting:

> Bring your counter of property, tribes, that he
>   may try in vain to count the property that is
>   to be given away by the great copper maker,
>   the chief.
> Go on, raise the unattainable potlatch-pole,
> For this is the only thick tree, the only thick
>   root of the tribes.

14

THE NOT-SO-VANISHING
RED MAN

WHAT OF THE INDIAN TODAY?

Where does he stand, in the world of jet planes and atomic energy, of television and supermarkets? Has he adapted to the breathless pace of change? Or has he, frightened and bewildered by the explosive spread of the white man and his ways, turned away to huddle in his villages and wait for the extinction of his race?

There are no easy ways of generalizing about the Indian in the twentieth century. Some Indians live in dreadful poverty; others are millionaires. Some still cling to the old ways; others are aggressive, alertly modern people. Some suffer from racial discrimination, others are community leaders. And some Indian tribes have vanished altogether.

The fate of the Indians has been a varied one, as we have seen. There are those who, like the Algonquians of the Atlantic Coast, simply disappeared. Others, such as the Five Civilized Tribes of the Southeast, were shifted wholesale from their ancestral lands and compelled to take up a new life elsewhere. The Apache, the Navaho, and the Indians of the Plains were rounded up and forced to abandon the entire pattern of their existence. Lucky ones like the Hopi and Zuni continued to live in the ways of their forefathers. Others, perhaps even luckier, made the headlong leap into the world of the invaders, adapting completely to the new order of things.

The conquest of the Americas was a sorrowful business. A new world of virgin land waited for conquest, and the conquerors came. Brutally, bloodily, they wrested the fertile continents from their inhabitants.

Could it have been otherwise? Could there have been "peaceful co-existence" between white man and red man? It hardly seems possible. How could Europeans, with their sense of property, of possession, allow nomads to live in their midst? How could the fabric of society hold together, when some "citizens" took wives and divorced them as they pleased, slew slaves to enhance their prestige, destroyed property, raided their neighbors?

To the settlers who came west in the years from 1600 to 1900, there was simply no choice. The Indians had to be turned into people who saw things in the European fashion. If they refused to learn the new ways, they would have to be exterminated for the common good of the majority. A typical expression of this attitude was voiced by Senator Pendleton of Ohio in the 1880's, during the debate on a controversial Indian affairs bill:

"They must either change their mode of life or they must die," the Senator declared. "We may regret it, we may wish it were otherwise, our sentiments of humanity may be shocked by the alternative, but we cannot shut our eyes to the fact that that is the alternative, and that these Indians must either change their modes of life or they will be exterminated. . . . We must stimulate within them to the very largest degree, the idea of home, of family, and of property. These are the very anchorages of civilization."

It does the Indians no good, at this late date, for us to debate the morality of our great-grandfathers. The Indians comprised a minority in the land that once was theirs: strangers in their own land, surrounded by aliens who regarded the intimate customs of the Indians with horror. The conflict between white man and Indian was a two-part battle: first, the struggle to take the land from the Indians; and second, the struggle to "cure" the Indians of their tribal customs and attitudes, and make them fit to enter the world of the white man.

The first part of the battle was largely over by 1880, much earlier in the East. Outnumbered and outfought, the Indians could not hope to resist any serious attempt at conquest. But the second half of the struggle was much more difficult, and it is only in our own day that something like a solution has been reached to the problem of what to do with the conquered Indians.

Our approach to that problem has shifted many times during the past two centuries. As a government

INDIAN RESERVATIONS TODAY

expert on Indian affairs, the late Felix Cohen, put it: "Like the miner's canary, the Indian marks the shifts from fresh air to poison gas in our political atmosphere; and our treatment of Indians, even more than our treatment of other minorities, reflects the rise and fall of our democratic faith."

For a while, it seemed as though there would be no Indian problem—that disease and despair would finish the red men off. When Columbus made his landfall, there were, the authorities agree, about a million Indians in North America. Four centuries later, the Indian population was no more than three hundred thousand. At a time when every nation in the world was undergoing vigorous population growth, the Indians were diminishing by more than two thirds.

The war of extermination waged by the white man played a part in this decline, of course. But for every Indian killed by a settler's bullet, five or six fell victim to the diseases that the Europeans brought with them. The historical record is a chilling one. Three thousand Caddo tribesmen dead of smallpox in 1691; one fourth of the Pawnee wiped out by cholera in 1871; thousands of Indians killed by smallpox in the Plains, 1781.

Intermarriage was a subtler way of disposing of the Indians. White settlers took Indian wives, widows of braves killed in warfare, and raised the children as whites. In the Northeast, particularly, whole tribes were devoured in this way. In a single generation, the old customs could be obliterated, old blood ties forgotten.

Poverty took its toll. Hungry people do not raise large families. Hungry children do not survive into adulthood. There was drunkenness, for the Indians had no liquor of their own, and with innocent eagerness became addicted to white man's firewater. And there was despair acting to cut down on population, too, for people who have lost everything, who have no future, do not seem to multiply the way a confident, dynamic group does.

So the Indian population shrank, helped along by the white man. By the end of the nineteenth century, those Indians who had survived the holocaust had been confined to reservations, except for a few hundred rebels. Most of the old treaties, between the United States and certain Indian tribes as sovereign nations, had been revoked on one pretext or another. Most of the Indian lands had been confiscated and turned over to white settlers. The Indians were little more than prisoners of war.

All that has changed today.

THE LOWEST EBB, for the Indians, was the period from 1869 to 1921, when they were compelled to live on reservations, and the plunder of their tribal lands went on enthusiastically. The greatest single blow to Indian hopes came in 1887, with the passage of the Dawes Allotment Act. This law provided that all Indian reservations were to be subdivided into individual plots of land to be assigned to individual Indians. They could not sell their allotments for twenty-five years.

Any surplus reservation land was to be bought by the government and made available to white settlers.

The purpose of the act was to break up the old system of community ownership of the land that was customary among Indians. By giving each Indian his own allotment of land, the government hoped to instill in him a sense of private property that would set him on the road toward thinking "like a white man."

The only road the Dawes Act set the Indian upon was the road to poverty. Shrewd, land-hungry white men moved in. They no longer had to deal with tribal elders, with a council of wise Indians, but with individual tribesmen. They worked out lease arrangements that speedily parted the Indians from their lands. Indians who had been herders needed thousands of acres of community land for grazing their flocks, and could not survive on allotments of 160 or 320 acres of land unsuitable for farming.

The fate of the Sisseton Indians, a Sioux tribe of South Dakota, shows vividly how the Dawes Act operated. Once the Sisseton had roamed free over thousands of square miles. In 1851 they had given over 40,000 square miles of Minnesota meadow land to the United States Government, and twenty years later had been persuaded to sell 11,000,000 acres of fertile land in the Red River Valley at ten cents an acre.

When the Dawes Act was passed in 1887, the two thousand Sisseton owned 918,000 acres of land. Under the allotment system, the tribe kept 308,000 acres, and the rest was sold to white settlers at $2.50 an acre. The

government agent in charge of the tribe wrote enthusiastically in 1892, "The red and white men will here-
after harvest their crops and herd their stock side by
side."

Although the Sisseton were among the most intelli-
gent and advanced of the Plains people, they were an
easy mark for white exploitation. They were persuaded
to sell or lease their land, and year by year their property decreased. By 1933, they had only about 110,000
acres of their original land left, and most of that had
been divided and subdivided through inheritance until few tribesmen owned more than a couple of acres.
Abysmal poverty prevailed. Three thousand Indians, in
1933, were trying to live on land that could support
no more than a few hundred. A Congressional subcom-
mittee, visiting the Sisseton reservation in 1946, called
their living conditions "one of the most disgraceful
situations in America." One Congressman called their
dwellings "worse than the places in which we keep
livestock."

To REMEDY ABUSES of this sort, a painfully slow
change in our attitudes evolved. Between 1887 and 1935,
when the Dawes Act was finally stricken from the
books, Indian-owned land had dwindled from 138,000,-
000 acres to 52,000,000, half of it desert or semidesert.
Half a dozen different legal mechanisms had been
used to push the Indians from their lands. They had
been paid pennies for land worth millions. Even when
they were paid fairly, they were given the money so

carelessly that they lost it. From 1915 to 1931, for example, the Osage Indians of Oklahoma were paid $265,-
000,000 in royalties from oil found on their lands. Two
thousand Indians, none of whom had any experience in
the ways of money, divided this immense kitty—but
were not protected in any way against the swarm of
promoters who moved in and deftly parted them from
their wealth, leaving them as poor as they had been
before.

It was a double problem. Some Indians were innocent as children, and needed to be guarded by the government. But others had earned the right to move into
the world of the white man as full-fledged citizens. How
could they at once be protected and be freed from
Federal control?

In 1924, Congress passed a law making the Indians
citizens of the United States, entitled to enjoy all the
privileges that citizenship entailed, including the right
to vote. Four years later came a monumental govern-
ment-sponsored study called *The Problem of Indian
Administration*, which laid bare the contradictions and
confusions of our Indian policy.

When Franklin Delano Roosevelt went to the White
House in 1933, one of the many sweeping reforms he
instituted was a complete overhaul of our Indian relations. The Indian Reorganization Act of 1934, sometimes called the Indian Bill of Rights, went a long way
toward undoing ancient wrongs.

It ended the allotment system. Indians might again
own land on a tribal basis. Surplus land not yet given

to whites would be restored to them. Tribes could organize as self-governing units under Federal protection. They could incorporate for business purposes. Funds were set up to provide loans to the Indians, enabling them to get started supporting themselves.

For a dozen years, that policy was in full force. Attitudes began to change again about 1950, in the latter days of the Truman Administration. And under President Eisenhower the government went a long way in the opposite direction.

The new policy was called "termination." The idea was to liberate the Indians from government control entirely, by breaking up the reservations and the tribal structure, and leaving the Indians on their own to sink or swim, just like any other citizens. This was to be done by act of Congress, "terminating" a tribe by passing a law declaring, in effect, that a given tribe no longer existed. All Indian rights would be taken away from the terminated tribe, land held in trust for the community would be divided, and tribal self-government would end.

Only a few tribes actually were terminated, such as the Klamath of Oregon and the Menominee of Wisconsin, both owners of large timber tracts sought by logging interests. After they had been terminated, these tribes were once again free to sell their lands, as they had been in the bad old days of the Dawes Act. But it soon became clear that this new policy, founded in the hope of setting the Indians free at last from their status as wards of the government, was a backward step. The year 1958 saw the Eisenhower Administration largely returning to the Roosevelt policies, and those policies are still in effect today.

WHAT, THEN, is the Indian's place in twentieth-century America?

It depends on the individual Indian. If he chooses, he can live the tribal life, pursuing those of the old ways that do not conflict too strongly with the white man's belief. (He is not free to keep slaves, to murder or scalp, to marry a dozen wives, or to go about naked. But he can practice his own farming or grazing techniques, dance his dances, pray to his own gods.)

Some Indians still live this way. But every Indian has the choice of leaving the reservation and entering the world of the white man. Contrary to popular belief, the reservations are not concentration camps for Indians. They do not *have* to live on them. Reservation life is an Indian's right and privilege, not a necessity. Thousands of Indians have left the reservations, have taken names like Jones or Thompson, and live the white man's life, working from nine to five, traveling home in the rush hour crush, sitting down after dinner to watch television for a while.

All Indians, on or off the reservation, can vote. They pay income taxes. They collect social-security benefits. The time will never come when we will "close the reservations and set the Indians free," because the reservations are not ours to close. That land belongs to the Indians. It is poor enough payment, indeed, for the continent we took away from them. The Indians on the reservations have certain special privileges. They pay no taxes on the land they own, or on the income they derive from it. They are usually subject to Federal, not state or local jurisdiction.

If we take a quick glance at what the Indians are doing in all parts of the United States, we see a general picture of activity and prosperity. There are some isolated pockets of poverty and despair, but the general view is more hopeful than it has been at any time since 1492.

The so-called Vanishing Red Man, for instance, is not vanishing at all. He is increasing, and increasing fast. There are about six hundred thousand full-blooded Indians in the United States today, less than half as many as lived here before Columbus, but half again as many as existed at the turn of this century. The population trend is definitely up. From 1940 to 1950, the birth rate among Indians under Federal jurisdiction increased by 16.7 per cent, while the birth rate of the population as a whole was growing only by 5 per cent. The most spectacular growth has been achieved by the Navaho. In 1868, when Kit Carson rounded them up, there were some six thousand of them. Today, there are some ninety thousand, more than a 1500 per cent increase in less than a century. They are by far the biggest Indian group in the nation; one Indian out of every seven today is a Navaho.

Birth-rate statistics tell only part of the story. If the Indians were multiplying without making progress economically, they would soon be in serious difficulties, but they are making strides toward self-sufficiency. Most Indian tribes are still terribly poor by white man's standards, but they are moving ahead rapidly.

Indians own almost 60,000,000 acres of land today, much of it rich in timber, oil, and metals. Their irrigated farmland alone amounts to more than 600,000 acres. The government-loan program has enabled many tribes to set up in business as herders or farmers on a handsome scale. Whereas the 1928 report on Indians declared: "They are not adjusted to the economic and social system of the dominant white civilization," a report today could point to prosperous and even wealthy Indians in many parts of the country. A few examples:

In northern California, a group of Pomo Indians borrowed $5,000 from the government in 1938 to buy a herd of dairy cows. By 1947, the loan had been repaid and the community had a surplus of $11,000.

In 1939, the Alaska community of Hydaburg borrowed $130,000 to finance the building of a salmon cannery. Eight years later, the loan was paid in full, and during that time the cannery had paid the community $200,000 in wages and $760,000 for fish caught by the tribe and sold to the plant.

In 1937, the Northern Cheyenne Indians of Montana went into the cattle business, and negotiated loans of $1,120,000 over a period of years. In six years, they paid off the loans and accumulated a surplus of $190,-000.

These dollar-and-cents stories show that the Indians of today are adapting to our world. There are records of hundreds of other Indian loans, and the Indians have proved to be the best credit risks in the country. Indian communities of farmers, ranchers, and even industrialists have come to dot the nation. Other Indians have gone into specialities, such as the famous Mohawk construction workers of New York. Some Indians have become extremely wealthy, thanks to the value of their oil or land holdings, and few have made the mistake of the Osage of 1915–31 in squandering their funds. Indians have been elected to high office, particularly in our Western states. John Nance Garner, a Texan of part Indian blood, served as President Franklin D. Roosevelt's first Vice-President. And on and on goes the story of Indian success.

There are debits, too: the Indians who have never understood our world, who still live in dirt and despondency and horrifying poverty. There is the fact that Indian life expectancy is still much shorter than that of the whites, that health on the reservations is not what it could be. And unknown to many of us, Indians are frequent victims of racial discrimination, not only in the South but elsewhere. Fiery crosses have been burned on the lawns of Indians who bought homes in white communities. Restaurants and hotels have turned Indians from their doors. All is not yet sweetness and light in the red man's world.

Nothing can ever undo the fact that the Indians were victims of conquest. No loans, no kindness, can heal that wound. We took not only their land but their freedom, their self-respect, their way of life.

The land cannot be returned, for our cities rise on it. Nor can the way of life come back. The Indians themselves have traveled too far on the path toward our civilization. Young men who have fought in our armies in wartime, who have seen machinery in action, who have experienced the twentieth century at first hand, cannot go back to the reservation to don paint and feathers. That life is largely gone, and where it has not yet disappeared, it soon will.

The Indian himself is still with us—very much so. In the words of Oliver La Farge, the novelist and anthropologist who devoted so much of his life to the Indians, "The Indians have not given up. They strive for the right to be themselves. Unlike any other American minority, they did not come here seeking freedom and a good life; they were here and had both until white men arrived and took these from them. They are our ultimate aristocrats. . . . They want tolerance, time, and reasonable opportunity, and they absolutely refuse to vanish."

Half a world once was theirs. In the continent that we call North America, they built a great many widely different civilizations, some of them, as we have seen, highly complex and advanced. Those civilizations, in the main, are gone. But we can look back, in sadness and in wonder, at the colorful, endlessly fascinating world of the Indians, in hope of capturing as best we can the flavor of that lost domain.

BIBLIOGRAPHY

UNACCOUNTABLE THOUSANDS of books and articles have been written about American Indians. Many of them are out of date; many are extremely specialized; and some are so rare as to be impossible to find. Still, anyone whose curiosity has been aroused by this book can go on to dozens of others, and then dozens more beyond those.

The list that follows includes books that I consulted most frequently in my own research, and some that I think will be useful to readers interested in following up in detail the subjects touched on with necessary brevity here. Books marked with a single asterisk are especially suited for young readers. Books marked with a double asterisk are technical in nature and recommended only for advanced research.

*Elizabeth C. Baity: *Americans Before Columbus,* The Viking Press; New York, 1951

John Bakeless: *Eyes of Discovery,* Peter Smith, Publisher; New York, 1961

*Gordon C. Baldwin: *America's Buried Past,* G. P. Putnam's Sons; New York, 1962

Ruth Benedict: *Patterns of Culture,* Houghton Mifflin Co.; Boston, 1934

Louis A. Brennan: *No Stone Unturned,* Random House; New York, 1959

John Collier: *Indians of the Americas,* W. W. Norton & Co.; New York, 1947

**Walter M. Daniels, ed.: *American Indians,* H. W. Wilson Co.; New York, 1957

*Edwin R. Embree: *Indians of the Americas,* Houghton Mifflin Co.; Boston, 1939

Harold S. Gladwin: *Men Out of Asia,* McGraw-Hill Book Co.; New York, 1947

*Bruce Grant: *American Indians Yesterday and Today,* E. P. Dutton & Co.; New York, 1958

**Robert F. Heizer, ed.: *Man's Discovery of His Past,* Prentice-Hall, Inc.; Englewood Cliffs, New Jersey, 1962

Alvin M. Josephy, Jr., ed.: *American Heritage Book of Indians,* American Heritage Publishing Co. Inc.; New York, 1961

**Alfred Kroeber: *Anthropology* (revised edition), Harcourt, Brace & World; New York, 1948

Kenneth MacGowan and Joseph A. Hester, Jr.: *Early Man in the New World* (revised edition), Doubleday & Co.; New York, 1962

D'Arcy McNickle: *They Came Here First,* J. B. Lippincott Co.; Philadelphia, 1949

*Alice Mariott: *The First Comers,* David McKay Co.; New York, 1960

**Paul S. Martin and others: *Indians Before Columbus,* University of Chicago Press; Chicago, 1947

*Paul Radin: *The Story of the American Indian,* Liveright Publishing Co.; New York, 1944

Vilhjalmur Steffanson: *Great Adventures and Explorations,* Dial Press; New York, 1947

*Matthew W. Stirling, ed.: *Indians of the Americas,* National Geographic Society; Washington, D. C., 1955

*Edwin Tunis: *Indians,* World Publishing Co.; Cleveland, 1959

Ruth M. Underhill: *Red Man's America,* University of Chicago Press; Chicago, 1953

**Clark Wissler: *The American Indian* (third edition), Peter Smith, Publisher; New York, 1950

Robert Silverberg

INDEX

246